DERVISH
— at the —
CROSS
ROADS

ESSENTIAL ESSAYS SERIES 73

ONTARIO ARTS COUNCIL
CONSEIL DES ARTS DE L'ONTARIO
an Ontario government agency
un organisme du gouvernement de l'Ontario

Canada Council   Conseil des arts
for the Arts   du Canada

Guernica Editions Inc. acknowledges the support
of the Canada Council for the Arts and the Ontario Arts Council.
The Ontario Arts Council is an agency of the Government of Ontario.
We acknowledge the financial support of the Government of Canada.

Wanda Waterman

DERVISH — at the — CROSS ROADS

A Soundquest Through
the First Two Decades
of the New Millennium

GUERNICA
EDITIONS
TORONTO • CHICAGO • BUFFALO • LANCASTER (U.K.)
2020

Michael Mirolla, editor
Cover and Interior Design: Rafael Chimicatti
Guernica Editions Inc.
287 Templemead Drive, Hamilton (ON), Canada L8W 2W4
2250 Military Road, Tonawanda, N.Y. 14150-6000 U.S.A.
www.guernicaeditions.com

Distributors:
Independent Publishers Group (IPG)
600 North Pulaski Road, Chicago IL 60624
University of Toronto Press Distribution,
5201 Dufferin Street, Toronto (ON), Canada M3H 5T8
Gazelle Book Services, White Cross Mills
High Town, Lancaster LA1 4XS U.K.

First edition.
Printed in Canada.

Legal Deposit – Third Quarter
Library of Congress Catalog Card Number: 2019949195
Library and Archives Canada Cataloguing in Publication
Title: Dervish at the crossroads : a soundquest through the first
two decades of the new millenium / Wanda Waterman
Names: Waterman, Wanda, author.
Series: Essential essays series ; 73. | Essential prose series ; 73.
Description: 1st edition. | Series statement: Essential prose ; 73
Essential essays series ; 73
Identifiers: Canadiana (print) 20190177934 | Canadiana (ebook) 20190177993
ISBN 9781771835008 (softcover) | ISBN 9781771835015 (EPUB)
ISBN 9781771835022 (Kindle)
Subjects: LCSH: Waterman, Wanda. | LCSH: Music journalists.
LCSH: Music—Social aspects—History— 21st century.
Classification: LCC ML3916 W38 2020 | DDC 780.9/05—dc23

Contents

Introduction:
story of a soundquest

The new world is as yet behind the veil of destiny.
In my eyes, however, its dawn has been unveiled.
 — Allama Muhammad Iqbal

The inexpressible proclamation has come, not from within and not
from without, not left, not right, not behind, not from before.

You say, 'What direction is that?' That direction where there is questing.
 — Jalal al-Din Rumi

This is the story of a soundquest, which is a kind of hero's journey but with a great soundtrack. A soundquest begins when you hear something mysteriously thrilling, something that drives you to keep tunnelling into the genre until you find the quintessence — *the* performance or *the* recording representing the culmination of listening pleasure for that genre. Experiencing this inevitably points out another musical direction.

My lifelong soundquest began with moving from one thrilling pop song to another, playing them to death until the tones went all tinny in my ears and had to be replaced by new songs that granted an equal or greater ecstasy.

As my tastes matured I moved from radio and television to vinyl LPs, choosing artists whose talents couldn't be nailed down to a spurious hit song but rather were meant to be enjoyed across ten tracks of an *album,* a thematically unified work whose smell, tactile qualities, liner notes, and broad expanse of graphic art enhanced the listening pleasure.

I wish I could say my soundquest was a triumph of educated taste, but when it came to music I was a shameless thrill seeker. The classical phase of my soundquest, for example, reached the fourth movement of Beethoven's Ninth; once I'd heard that I continued to listen to classical music but not as ravenously.

In 2005 I started paying homage to my soundquest by writing regularly about music, in print, for webzines, and for my blog. Writing about music was, I thought, a way of paying it back for the light it had brought to my dark hours. I hadn't written many articles before I'd conceived the idea of one day creating a book. As time went on I thought of this book as a way of redeeming all the time spent creating "disposable" writing. The book I imagined would, I hoped, grant a little permanence to my insights and those I was gleaning from the artists I interviewed.

As a music writer I sought out new recordings that I found original, authentic, and delightful – music I thought might edify and inspire compassionate creators. I naïvely hoped that promoting this kind of music might raise the sea levels of love, joy, and beauty in the world, even if only just a little.

I pretended there was no such thing as a music industry, a hits chart, or a superstar. My goal wasn't to find the next big thing but rather to follow the most stirring music wherever it might lead me. My writing was no more than an extension of my soundquest.

Why hadn't I become a musician myself? My music teacher in high school was surprised when I told him I wouldn't be majoring in music at university, and I was surprised at his surprise. He had apparently seen me as having a natural aptitude, but he'd never said so and neither had anyone else. Besides, I lacked the degree of extraversion necessary to placing oneself in the public eye. I was a writer, and music was just what I did to keep me happy. Music entered my poetry by means of the pulsing iambic rhythm I'd copied from Poe, an archaic poetic time signature that ensured my work would take up only marginal space in late twentieth century poetry. I also incorporated music into my writing by writing about it.

Eventually I began searching for the material that had inspired my idols Beethoven, John Coltrane, Joni Mitchell, Captain Beefheart, Neil Young, Johnny Cash, Led Zeppelin, *et al,* that is, the music that had informed their highest achievements.

My soundquest took on a larger scope, becoming an attempt to get at the heart of music itself, to find out what music *means*. This is what came over me toward the end of the 20th century and what has dictated my life choices since then. *What is music and where does it get its power?* I had a hunch back then that music might be part of Leonard Cohen's "crack in everything" – the crack that lets the light in – but I needed more evidence.

Looking back, it's very odd that it didn't matter to me that my poems, plays, and essays rarely brought anyone any real happiness. Writing was no bed of roses for me either. I slaved away at it for years in the belief that one day I would be understood and appreciated, that my ideas would provide just a little more clarity to the world.

But providing pages of print in the new millennium was a thankless task. Not many of us, it seemed, had time to read. Even I had to admit that it had been years since I'd had the luxury of taking my time with a good book; the struggle for survival took up so much time that the only books I read were those I was reviewing, and any other reading had to be snatched randomly in waiting rooms or on bus trips. Even now much of my reading comes through audio books listened to while cooking and tidying. It's not my favourite way of consuming books, but there's no time for curling up in an armchair with a cup of tea in one hand and a weighty tome in the other.

Everyone in my circle who worked shared my dilemma. Since the sixties wages had slowly dropped to below the cost of living and employers had steadily demanded more and more from workers than workers could supply. Those of us who'd entered "gig" culture, no longer salaried employees but rather free agents in search of clients, had seen our hourly wages slowly dwindle along with the mounting competition. If few had time to read anymore, even fewer could afford to buy new books. The time crunch had resulted in many of us returning to a more primitive condition in which words weren't read but heard, and online writing wasn't so much studied as scanned.

This may explain why my poetry readings have garnered far more positive responses than have invitations to read my poems. Perhaps the ancients had something on us with their recitations of odes and epics around the evening fire. And it's not just the rat race that's making audio books so popular: As a means of delivering words to an audience, the human voice beats print hands down.

Print, as valuable as it is for disseminating information (as well as for highlighting and margin notes), can actually dilute the intensity of certain events, especially when it describes them literally. I didn't really want to know scientifically why this was, but I did want to follow this idea where it led. At that moment I couldn't quite get used to the idea of using my own voice to express my thoughts – that was to come later.

One important thing I learned during these two decades was that the conditions of our time make it harder for us to see ourselves as points along a series of evolutions. We're not living through any revolutionary musical genre. Instead, all of music, from the beginning of written and recorded music, is now present to us. For today's listener ancient Greek hymns are as accessible as Lady Gaga's latest hit. This availability grants a new vantage point from which to appreciate musical genres, freed from the judgments present within their original historical contexts.

A lot of research went into this book, but its theme and methods are more mystical than scholarly, my goal having been to understand why I found this era in music so fundamentally different from what had preceded it and what this told me about the nature of music itself.

The musicians and composers I've interviewed have confirmed many of my instincts and pointed me in new directions, but some of their answers confused me and compelled me to go on digging. This book draws much from these interviews, and whenever you see the word "interview" and a year after a quotation from an artist you'll know that this quote came from an interview I conducted with them, in person or by email, telephone, Skype, or Facetime.

You'll notice that the book is written not in a sequential historical line but in a kind of swirly-whirly pattern, hopping back and forth between 2000 and 2020 and often referring to a more distant past. So go ahead and open it anywhere; reading it that way seems strangely appropriate.

You may not see much logic in my argument, and for good reason. The first time I heard Slavoj Zizek holding forth I thought, *What's wrong with this guy? He has no system. He doesn't define his terms. There's no ideology or dogma to accept or reject. He just keeps talking until a few things start to become clear.* I've since completely come around to this method of exposition. It seems somehow more honest, even more edifying. Thank-you, Zizek.

Earlier versions of some of the graphics and passages in this book have appeared in webzines and on my blog, *The Mindful Bard*. But here they're better and make more sense.

Many thanks to the Athabasca University Student Union Webzine *The Voice* for running my articles and interviews over the years; your patronage went far toward making this book a reality. I must thank my musical friends for putting several collaborations on hold until I finished the book. I also want to thank my husband Ahmed for bringing me to the Sahara Desert in 2014. And of course I'm deeply grateful to all the musical artists who took the time to share their thoughts about music.

I hope my story encourages you to take a good look at your own soundquest, if you're on one, or to go on a soundquest if you haven't yet begun. You have only to gain.

The weirdest, most transcendent period in music's history

"Mr. Tambourine Man" in the year 2000

At 10 p.m., January 17, 2000, the group home's clients were comfy in their beds when Catherine and I swung out the acoustics for a quiet jam session. We sat on cushions, and sliding around on the floor beside us were our ragged old chord and lyric sheets, some typed, some handwritten.

Know this one? "Tambourine Man." Yay. Love it. But not in that key. I can do the chords, but it's too high to sing. What about G? Okay, play it in G with the capo on the third fret and we'll sing it down an octave.

Thus we reeled, disappearing in the smoke rings of our minds.

Pied Pipers

Pierre Elliott Trudeau had just died. The Liberal Party's Jean Chrétien was prime minister of Canada, and warmonger George W. Bush had just beaten environmentalist Al Gore to the American presidency. It was long before I'd begun seeing ruling parties as forecasts of musical climate change, but now I know why so much kickass punk music emerged during those years. In 2009 I compared the Canadian punk band Fucked Up to the Pied Piper of Hamelin:

> You can almost hear somebody saying, 'You failed to give me what you promised, so I'm taking your children.'
>
> It seems the children are following, entranced, in droves. Fucked Up's career has so far straddled the two George W. Bush terms, and their music is a radically fitting response to an era notorious for expensive exercises in futility, including broken deals with rat catchers.

Just as it had done in the seventies and eighties, punk rock was easing the déjà vu hopelessness, the shocked realization that the ideals of the sixties were being hammered into the ground. Punk was supposed to be rescuing those writhing in life's corrosion, delivering them from "the twisted reach of crazy sorrow," but somehow punk no longer held the same consoling and affirming power or the sense of freak solidarity it had had in the seventies.

No longer about trends

> During tough times in countries, the '70s in the UK with punk rock,
> the Reagan era, the '90s grunge ... all of this was reactive music.
> — Rishi Dhir of Elephant Stone, interview, 2016

I agree with Dhir; the music of the seventies, eighties, and nineties was largely reactive. And so was music in the year 2000, but in 2000 people were no longer concerned about being true to current trends, at least not in the way they'd been in the sixties. Catherine and I didn't have any problem singing songs whose heyday had long passed. We could sing old Bob Dylan songs – it was okay. It was all there for us now, not like when each new music scene pre-empted everything that had come before and promised to hang around forever.

In singing, "Hey, hey, my, my, rock and roll will never die," Neil Young had thrown out a rather reckless challenge. Looking around us today we can see that perhaps rock and roll will be around until Doomsday, but it certainly will never again hold a monopoly on the ears of the young masses. In the twentieth century, chamber orchestras had had to yield centre stage to jazz bands that had had to yield the stage to rock, and then rock's turn had come. The big difference with rock is that when the bells began to toll it had had to move aside not to make way for one new genre but rather for all the music ever recorded.

Back to the group home. Rachel had just arrived, opening the door to let the sea breeze leak in. Behind her blond bouffant stood dark silhouettes of pines and the moon's path on the Bay of Fundy. That was what *we* saw. She was later to describe the sight of us with our guitars to another worker thus:

"My God, I thought I'd walked into a sixties love-in!"

She'd been there

In mentioning the word "love-in" Rachel had been referring back to a "scene." Which scene? The scene in which the following had occurred:

On a Friday in October in 1965 a girl named Deborah in the Haight-Ashbury district of San Francisco cashed her waitressing cheque and went to the record shop to pull a copy of Bob Dylan's newly pressed

Bringing it All Back Home from the hands of the clerk just as he was about to slide it into the D section of the "Folk" bin. She took the album back to her crowded loft, listened a few times, and taught herself how to play "Mr. Tambourine Man," having recognized it as the most significant song on the album.

Barefoot, wearing a flowery mini-dress, and filled with elation, Deborah took her guitar down to the street and played the song again and again for the wandering prep school, grad school, and old school gypsies, all high on life, acid, and weed.

For the rest of her life the memory of this event justified Deborah's existence. Whatever failures and losses were to come, she could say she'd been there and done that. For one enchanted evening she'd followed a pied piper, inviting the other children to come along.

For Catherine and me there were no pied pipers. There was just us.

It was just as well; the handful of pipers selected to lead the youth back to the garden during the sixties had rejected the role anyway, and for good reason. Artists aren't leaders. Music does change things, but don't ask musicians to take the reins in any new political direction. Besides, only in the sixties could someone believe she could change the world by singing on a street corner.

> ... a lesson has been taught which will not be learned. It is that one should not try to found a revolution on musicians; because the delicate instrument of their body can all too easily be damaged, they are all prone to desert.
> —Grace Slick[1]

Dylan, for example, had never asked to be the poster child for the radical resistance. He'd been turned off by efforts to make him the mouthpiece for the anti-war movement just as he'd resented attempts to deconstruct his songs and dictate their meanings.[2]

---

1   Peter Doggett: *There's a Riot Going On: Revolutionaries, Rock Stars, and the Rise and Fall of the '60s*

2   Peter Doggett: *There's a Riot Going On: Revolutionaries, Rock Stars, and the Rise and Fall of the '60s*

The Beatles had been seen as trendsetters, but they'd simply been followers who'd brought certain alternative ideas, practices, and styles to public awareness. Besides, their status as social leaders was shaky enough to wobble when their guru was outed as a perv.

"We're human," John Lennon said, not letting the egg on his face keep him from popping his eyes sarcastically at reporters.

Not even the soft-spoken Saskatonian Joni Mitchell, her dreamy fairy manner aped by flower children from San Francisco to Cornerbrook, had been willing to lead the "stardust, golden, million-year-old carbon" back to the garden. She'd condemned greed and environmental destruction but had refused most requests to play for charitable causes. Despite her lifelong revulsion to patriarchy, efforts to get Mitchell to speak out for feminism were usually ignored. She felt that feminists dismissed the feminine principles and practices she embraced; she was all about personal integrity and only as much social concern as that dictated. She had a grudge against the world that was now demanding her help, so she wasn't about to jump when they snapped their fingers.

We'd learned a lesson, or ought to have: Never subjugate art to power.

The optimism of the Woodstock attendees and street corner singers questioned itself after violence erupted at the Altamont Festival in 1969, and much of the counterculture shifted its allegiance away from British rock and toward North American roots: blues, bluegrass, folk, Cajun, early jazz, and old-timey music, among others. The back-to-the-land movement gained steam. Musicians and listeners in other countries followed suit by turning back to their own folk traditions.

Rock had made the politicized folk music movements of the late fifties and early sixties look hokey. Few were willing to bear that torch again, which meant the new Americana wouldn't be a soapbox for any specific political agenda but instead a searching of its origins for a new sense of identity. Rock looked dark, sinister, and worse; it was getting harder to deny the degree to which it was, in all its rebelliousness, the sanitized product of a handful of suits gunning for their next million.

The counterculture's abandonment of the connection between music and social concern, while leaving creativity vulnerable to corporate influence, at the same time allowed for deeper personal explorations. This in turn lead to a more focused compassion and a desire to use art to speak to suffering in a healing way, via confession and empathy. None had proven better equipped to travel in this new direction than Canadians Leonard Cohen, Joni Mitchell, Neil Young, Gordon Lightfoot, and Buffy Sainte Marie.[3] But just as Jane Austen's high art had inspired countless cheap romance novels so too did the work of these master singer-song-writers inspire years of mediocre mimicry from their admirers.

In the now

Catherine and I weren't playing "Mr. Tambourine Man" for the gypsies – not in the year 2000. The gypsies who'd flocked to Nova Scotia in the sixties were now altered beyond recognition, increasingly bewildered at the ways in which they were becoming just like their parents. We were, however, in a position to grasp the meaning of the lyrics better than Haight-Ashbury Deborah could have, and only because of all that had passed since 1965.

While we were still trying to make sense of our own pasts, we were no longer inclined to "forget about today until tomorrow." We weren't so likely to dismiss the music of earlier eras the way folkies and rockers of the sixties had dismissed Louis Armstrong's music as irrelevant es-capism. Our years of struggle, loss, bad romances, addictions, therapy, and meditation had brought us to a fuller understanding of the value of "living in the now."

We'd both been born at the very tail end of the baby boom. As teen-agers we hadn't been willing to worship the same pied pipers the flower children had followed into their golden years. They were still holding them up as beacons for us, their younger siblings, babysitters, children, and friends' children. Sure, we *liked* all that music, we *respected* it, but it wasn't ours. It didn't speak to our experience of having been born into a Bacchic culture but forced to grow up in a Machiavellian one. For that we'd needed punk rock.

I'd observed that by the year 2000 the youthful practice of lifting musical performers to pantheon status, sacrificing clothing allowances on their records and looking to them for divine guidance, was getting

---

3   *Whispering Pines: The Northern Roots of American Music from Hank Snow to the Band*, by Jason Schneider, 2009 ECW Press

old. As star worship lost momentum so did the idea that one musical genre should fill the airwaves. Rhythm and blues and hip hop were dominating the radio and record sales, but record purchases and radio listening were happening less and less. There was plenty of original new music, yet the best of it was uncategorized, and its creators wouldn't touch stardom with a barge pole.

The industry didn't get it. Instead of recognizing that there were fewer idol-worshipers, they assumed the world just needed more idols. Television shows like the aptly named *American Idol* and its spinoffs attempted to address the star gap in the most contrived way imaginable, by auditioning all over the country and using a process of elimination to find the country's next superstar so they could pour their ample resources into developing his or her career. It was like King Solomon scouring the kingdom for his next queen. But no Esther was forthcoming; as entertaining as the show was, it made no new contributions to musical culture. And watching the music industry selecting and grooming someone to represent the voice of the country's youth showed just how ludicrous the idea of manufactured success had been from the beginning.

Retro since the nineties

I find music in general (post nineties) has been retro ever since the 'grunge' movement. In the fifties and sixties we had jazz and rock and roll. Then the seventies came out of flower power, stadium rock to punk, jazz to fusion. In the eighties we had new wave and heavy metal. Style and music and fashion were intertwined with new sounds. That has vanished over the last 20 years.

Perhaps electronic music is the one style that has evolved, but as for 'popular' music, it's been chasing its tail for quite some time. Iconic artists and groups are few and far between; there are not many (if any) that can reach the impact that the Led Zeppelins or the Bowies had in the past, let alone the longevity. It's kind of like trying to invent a new colour.

— Steve Ludwik, co-owner of Death of Vinyl
(Montreal record store), interview 2017

The situation owes something to changes in demographics in the west. While populations in other countries have continued to maintain a balance of age groups, baby boomers in Europe and North America have dominated other age groups. The cohort whose buying habits once made record executives slobber all over themselves bidding for the massive sales they generated have grown older and are now consuming every musical genre imaginable.

The percentage of adolescents and young adults having shrunk, so has the commercial impetus to get behind (or manufacture) cultural movements.

In my memory the last significant movement was the punk uprising of the late seventies and early eighties. Youth who'd been put to sea by dysfunctional families and the dissolution of mental health services lived high-risk lives and generated music that screamed angst, disgust, rage, and horror. When survivors got older and were forced to work for a living they often rubbed elbows with former flower children. Together the former punks and hippies had a measure of cultural clout that added to the eclecticism of musical demand. They were entering middle and old age at a time when all their favourite music could be available to them, much of it free. Leaps in information technology had allowed sound sharing and collaborations to happen around the globe, continuously. The results were dizzying. Genres had always mixed, but technology had speeded up that process like nobody's business.

Back in the thirties radio introduced Hawaiian slack-key guitar to American country singers, who quickly incorporated their version of it into their ballads and hurtin' songs.

The phonograph let white musicians hear "race" records, allowing jazz techniques and chord progressions to influence traditional Western classical and popular songs.

Later on television became a portal of new sounds generated for itself alone: series themes, movie music, and programs like *The Archies, The Monkees* and *The Partridge Family,* that showed my generation from an early age how delightfully freeing rock music could make us feel. Television was our introduction to mainstream genres as well as little-known subgenres that made it onto the screen almost miraculously (e.g. hill country blues singer Jesse Mae Hemphill's appearance on *Mr. Rogers' Neighborhood*).

But nothing was to compare to the new millennium, when the mp3 and the Web brought us ease of access to much of recorded music. This technology also enabled ordinary people to make their own recordings. The personal computer was rising to tasks formerly carried out by costly and well-equipped recording studios, and nothing had ever held a candle to how quickly home-recorded music could now be shared.

Retrospect is enlightening: new musical pioneers

One beautiful early outcome of this ease of mixing and recording is Conrad Praetzel's alt country electronica (my description, not his). Just as everything was beginning to turn retro, Praetzel began remixing old American field recordings and adding his own instrumentation to draw out the essence of the music. He described how he put it all together:

> Finding that first link with the vocal source is one of the most rewarding parts of working from these old field recordings. When it does work you feel like you've opened a door into some place no one else has been. The rest of the arrangements just sort of fall into place.
> — Conrad Praetzel, interview, 2009

The best new musical pioneers are on a soundquest; they have a primal sound in their heads that they pursue with all their might, using all the tools technology puts at their disposal. The spirit of music itself is just as vibrant in these new works inspired by the past as it is for those who claim to make tunes up out of whole cloth.

Why? Because we now have a unique vantage point for viewing the past in a way that the people living through that past could never have imagined.

Emerging in 2005, the music of the Carolina Chocolate Drops would have been called "alt country" had it not been so true to the era they were revisiting. Southern string band music is a kind of niche genre dug up from the past and given an astonishing new life by this group of erudite musicians, who bring it to those born too late to have caught it the first time around.

For cofounder Dom Flemons it was Bob Dylan's music that had led him into the winding vaults of bygone sounds. Rhiannon Giddens, the other founding member, began her soundquest with a classical career that moved into contra dancing and Celtic music. Clearly a band of masters, the Drops embraced tradition just enough to skirt academic rigidity, have fun, and nurture the creative development of this amazing style of music. Flemons explained:

> 'Riro's House' isn't a traditional arrangement. Hubby and Rhiannon are playing the main arrangement that she and I learned from Joe Thompson, and I added snare drum and bass drum in the fife and drum style. While this may not seem like a big difference, these subtleties are the way we give the music our personal stamp, which is truly the way to make a modern song out of a traditional song – taking material from the past and making something new out of it.
> —Dom Flemons, interview 2012

Taking the old and making it new again is sometimes dismissed as shallow cultural reenactment or, worse, a reckless mishmash of creative self-indulgence, when in fact it's always been essential to cycles of musical development. To a large extent this has been a feature of rising importance in the new musical landscape, and it didn't just happen in roots music.

Dinuk Wijeratne was deeply inspired by Mozart but doesn't base his work on the master's. Rather he bases his own composition on, as he puts it, "the concept," echoing Jacques Maritain's[4] assertion that a work of art dictates the terms of its own development:

> I love combining musical influences. I'm basically an eclectic in every way. I was taught by eclectics and I only seem to work with eclectics.
>
> But I never do synthesis for its own sake. I never think consciously, 'this needs to be mixed with that.' Ultimately everything is concept-driven, so if I think something needs a certain element for the sake of the concept and just because I'm moved by it, then I'll use it.
> —Dinuk Wijeratne, interview 2010

---

4   Maritain, Jacques, *Art and Scholasticism, and the Frontiers of Poetry,* Scribner 1962

Raï artist Rachid Taha also embraced eclecticism and multicultur-
alism with a passion, applying it to his entire life and worldview.

> I live in a very multicultural world, and I've always been curious.
> I like discovering things. I like Western art. I like to listen to Arabic
> music, Italian music, and American rock and roll. I love to listen to
> Johnny Cash, Elvis Presley, and Richie Havens. I'm really interested
> in the cinema, especially Japanese cinema (I love Kurosawa). I've
> always liked Jim Ford. Again, my curiosity ends up feeding my music.
> — Rachid Taha, interview 2013

You could argue that eclecticism represents a kind of overarching
"scene" that has existed for centuries and is only now coming to the
fore, seeping into the culture at large and finding itself among its peers
the world over.

Music has evolved from a linear path to a kind of vortex that we swirl
into, a vortex within which all genres are now with us, cycling and going
forward at the same time.

Has music ever been pure?

Game changer

Today we can hear compositions by dead composers interpreted by world-renowned artists, live or in recordings. We can find sheet music and tinkle away on our pianos along with Ludovico Einuadi. We can pretend to be Aretha Franklin on karaoke. We can carry massive music libraries around with us on our mobile devices.

On some level this changes the game completely. It makes musical consumption a far more individualized affair, listeners not so much fans of large-scale movements as members of myriad small cult followings. It spoils us a little, making us less patient and more particular. Moreover, musical artists today have to compete with those bygone artists whose work stands up under endless repetitions. This doesn't erase the need for new music, but it does challenge it a little, which is why the present surfeit of new recordings may have a harder time finding listeners.

Not with a line but a vortex

But back to the vortex for a moment. The spiral image represents a mindset less focused on current trends and more concerned with all of music, which turns joyfully around us wherever we may be, guiding us along it. This has lead to a greater mindfulness and a speeded-up eclecticism. Contrary to my Luddite intuition, it's made musical experience that much more immediate.

Is this a good thing? You bet it is.

One side effect of the move from linear to vortical musical progression is the declining significance of the avant-garde. There'll always be an avant-garde, no doubt, but as is the case with much of what's called "alternative" rock these days, after a while it sounds all-of-a-piece. It's hard to be innovative once innovation has become the order of the day, and what deliberately jars and jolts the ears might as easily be lounge or polka as John Cage. Avant-garde sound experiments continue, but no one seems offended by them anymore, so why bother?

Dismiss no more

Today we turn on the radio, visit a record shop, peruse local concert listings, or go online to find a smorgasbord of musical works composed as early as the dark ages. Each musical dish has its intelligent devotees, so we can no longer dismiss bubblegum, house music, disco, polka, smooth jazz, or Strauss waltzes as passé. Passé is now passé. Intellectual college students today can't dismiss disco as we did when I was a student, since David Byrne admitted that his compositions for the Talking Heads were inspired by disco rhythms.

Retro jazz queen Janet Klein proudly rejects the *au courant*:

> For me, the idea of 'newer is better' just does not compute. Basically I bumped off the road of my discontent, trying to find what I did like, because there were so many things around me that left me feeling unhappy or like a Martian.
>
> I seem to have the taste of an old lady. It took years to figure this out. But I kept at it and stayed with the things that I found pleasure in. Eventually, it completely took hold and I felt like, 'Hey, now I can draw others into my bubble!'
> — Janet Klein, interview 2010

We can access any age, any musical development, right now, reviving the tradition and adding new things to it, and though any sound can be disliked, none can be tossed – all can and do inspire new music.

If serious music lovers regard this new vortical reality with fear and trepidation it's only because it's so new and changing so quickly that it's hard to predict where it's headed. Hard, but not impossible.

Postmodernism

On one fine day back in the nineties I was having a conversation with a woman of both Native American and African American descent. For some reason the topic had come around to how people on the West coast were different from people on the East coast. I shared my opinion that Westerners tended to be more adventurous, individualistic, extroverted, egotistical even, than their reserved, stolid cohorts in the East.

"I suppose it all comes down to history," I mused. "When the European settlers started arriving, the more traditional, communal types put down roots in the East and stayed there, while the more curious, brave, and creative pioneer types moved West."

I was thinking in a purely linear fashion: This, that, and the other thing are happening now because of the historical timeline that lead up to them.

She smiled gently and replied, "I suppose I see it from the perspective of my own ancestors."

I woke with a jolt. Of course – her ancestors had arrived from the West and moved East. Others has arrived from the southwest and moved north. The rest had been brought by force to the east and had thereafter moved north and west. Crediting colonial history with making Westerners creative but uncivilized and for making Easterners disciplined but dull just didn't apply. You only had to talk to a First Nations person or a descendent of African slaves – or a new immigrant, for that matter – to know that such generalizations were absurd.

Postmodernism is realizing that my history isn't all history, my people aren't all people, and my values aren't necessarily the only ones that matter. Postmodernism is not just the road, it's also the wheel, going forward while ceaselessly turning. That wheel is made up of all of us.

Postmodernism is sometimes described as a rejection of linear thinking, and my experience has shown this to be a reasonable thing to do. Rejecting linear thinking can grant us an enhanced ability to understand reality, progressing to a thought process that's more like a mindmap or a Venn diagram than a timeline. Needless to say this completely changes the concept of "progress" as defined by modernists. Even though it was the modernists who'd first postulated social equality as an essential ingredient of a just society, they'd failed to recognize the nonlinear nature of human development and interaction.

No external measure of truth

In addition to respecting multiple viewpoints, another important element of postmodernity is the questioning of vertical (or diagonal) power structures. Few can now say with any conviction that parents, teachers, churches, the justice system, governments, or, for the purposes of our present exploration, record companies, must be obeyed without question.

Although the postmodern individual keeps an open mind, she sees herself as the highest authority on her own truth. In a way this isn't far from the beliefs of our ancestors; even those who preached obedience to the monarch were doing so out of an idea that existed within their own skulls, a personal conviction that leaders had a divine right to lead and that our divine task as underlings was to obey. Since then our minds have changed only in that they trust themselves a little more.

Carl Jung, among others, pointed out that the only means we have for discerning truth is the human brain, a highly fallible instrument. As much as we long for truth, we may be incapable of finding it. Single-mindedly pursuing truth results in enterprises like the construction of the Tower of Babel, where communication itself becomes so confounded that humans are no longer united in their efforts. Our efforts are better spent in a search of *meaning*, because meaning, it appears, is something the human mind is specially equipped to discern.

What this means for postmodernists is that individuals can't easily be compelled to trust representatives of power who claim to be purveyors of truth, because not only are authority figures fallible, the very concept of "truth" is in question.

In its ideal condition postmodernism is a perfect balance between collectivism and individualism, inspiring a social model in which every individual viewpoint is given equal weight and no one viewpoint is given center stage. A tall order, but aiming for it does engender an interesting array of attitudes, ranging from a more sincere valuing of our fellow creatures to a sense, on the dark side, that since no one matters more than another, no one really matters at all. There's ample evidence that music enables the first attitude and that human vice maintains the second.

> ME: If you had an artistic mission statement, what would it be?
> GERLACH: To inspire all to live in the fullest expression of their inner divinity in whatever art form they like.
> ME: Do you feel that artists have an obligation to straighten the world out a little?

GERLACH: I think musicians have been the foundation of finding or losing one's sanity since the epoch of musical expression. The
world should become more musical and then it would all straighten
itself out naturally.
— Rachel Gerlach of Fable Cry, interview, 2018

My own soundquest had taught me the same principles: Humans
are inherently divine, and music can help us find our inner sacredness.

Forging new old trails

"Starmaker machinery"

> You know I'd go back there tomorrow
> But for the work I've taken on
> Stoking the star maker machinery
> Behind the popular song
>   — Joni Mitchell, from the song "Free Man in Paris"

In 2007, just before being dropped from the lineup, *American Idol* runner up Melinda Doolittle went backstage and sighed to the camera, "I'm tired." You could tell she meant it to her very soul.

The race is not to the swift. Melinda was not your typical *American Idol* contestant. She wasn't a pop star; she was a true artist, as sensitive and resonant as a Stradivarius violin. She'd given her all and then some, and the gruelling demands of the show were doing her in. Simon Cowell later claimed she should have won, and he was right. She *would* have won had the contest been based on talent alone and not on how well a performer could submit to the inhuman demands of the corporate world.

Corporate intelligence

Several popular science fiction novels and films have posed the question, "What if artificial intelligence were to develop its own consciousness and take over the world?" The fictional consensus is that machines nearly always turn out to be hostile to human concerns.

I'm still not convinced that artificial intelligence, by nature no more than a tool of the human mind, might ever become a mind in itself; it's like saying a hammer might one day become a hand. There is however a type of nonhuman entity that can take on a mind of its own and even demonstrate a primitive self-awareness. The agents of this body are so frighteningly self-interested and anti-human at times that you can practically insert them into the roles of the "Agents" in *The Matrix*.

I'm talking of course about large corporations. The scariest thing about them is that so many in so many countries are working so hard to ensure that these bodies control every aspect of our lives, justifying their efforts with flawed economic theories. Naturally music isn't exempt from the influence of a being whose raison d'être is to raise profits for shareholders, a being who demonstrates resentment when anyone demands that it value life above profits – a being exemplifying the darkest elements of the masculine.

Singer Bonnie Whitmore had this to say about what this means for female music makers:

> It's not easy to be in this business as an artist, period. The industry side is lazy. They want what will help their "bottom line," but their formula is outdated and doesn't really create anything, just repackages the same sound in pretty wrapping. When the quality of music suffers, its seems to weigh more heavily on women in part because the music industry is run by men who are more visually than audibly stimulated. That in a nutshell is what the problem is with the music biz, period. Sexism is still strong and outspoken in this and many industries, and there's no point in denying that. I do think we are at a turning point, but that has more to do with women supporting fellow women and likeminded men who can see past the genitalia to the quality of sound and song.
> — Bonnie Whitmore, interview 2016

Tax Man

In 1966 Harold Wilson of the Labour Party proposed a tax of 95% on Britain's highest salaries. It's come down a bit since then, but the Beatles were among Britain's highest earners, and George Harrison was so irked at the measure that he wrote "Tax Man."

It's amazing that the protest of a rich man at having to pay tax didn't knock the Beatles off their pedestals as youth culture icons, as distrust of the rich was an essential component of youth culture. But youth culture icons were, it seems, the only ones whose wealth went unbegrudged. The Beatles had come from the working class, so good for them if they made a few extra quid, and phooey on the tax man.

But when Neil Young and Donovan showed up at the 1970 Isle of Wight Festival in fancy cars[5] there was a wave of grumblings, especially since many had thought the concert would be free and there'd been a big discrepancy between how rich and poor had been treated during the festival. [6]

Folksingers had been seen as specially representative of a widespread rejection of luxury and social status. Trouble is, many of the new folk-singers, essentially singer-songwriters and not folksingers at all, weren't very aware of this, and the music moguls certainly couldn't be counted on to promote simple living.

But it wasn't ignorance that drove industry execs to swathe their counterculture clients in luxury like noodles in butter. It's the trick of every wealthy parent whose child decides to become a communist: Get them used to the finer things – the best clothes, cars, restaurants, schools, trips abroad. Refine their tastes. Ensure they'll accept nothing but the best, wrinkling their noses at anything substandard. Let them develop their own tastes, for sure, and admire them loudly for choosing organic this and handmade that. Eventually they'll figure out that all of these things cost more than they can afford as proletarian revolutionaries, but by then it'll be too late for them to change their consumer habits. And the longer they live in ease and splendour the better equipped they'll be to find the weaknesses in Marx's arguments.

A similar thing happens when musical artists ascend. Not only does the music industry want their stars to be conspicuously rich, they want their fans to admire their wealth, equating prosperity with all that's good, true, and beautiful so they'll continue giving up their hard-earned money to support it.

It was awareness of this sad process that fuelled the first wave of punk rock in the late seventies, but big money knew better than to hang back;

---

5   Doggett, Peter, *There's a Riot Going On: Revolutionaries, Rock Stars, and the Rise and Fall of the '60s*, 2008 Canongate

6   Schneider, Jason, *Whispering Pines: The Northern Roots of American Music from Hank Snow to the Band*, 2009 ECW Press

garage band screamers had recording contracts before you could say "bugger off, wanker." But the punks were a little more reluctant to succumb to days of wine and roses; their very aesthetic, if you could call it that, rejected the American dream and all the bollocks that went with it.

The punks conspicuously rejected quality and good taste. Thumbing their noses at the hippies' worship of all things natural, Cyndi Lauper extolled the praises of linoleum, Sean Penn went to live in a trailer, and high school girls spent hours each morning brutalising their hair and perfecting their Elvira makeup.

In a roundabout way this period of stubborn resistance played a role in the fragmentation of commercial music and the weakening of the music industry's control after 2000.

An ancient table

My iMac sat on an ancient table with chipping royal blue paint. On this table I made recordings, conducted interviews, created comic strips, and wrote articles. The window before me looked out onto a birch spinney that hummed with the songs of minute creatures occasionally shocked into silence by the lumberings of larger ones. I made little distinction between the music coming from iTunes and the music wafting in from outdoors. Sometimes when I wanted to meditate I'd count the different streams of sound I was hearing, picturing them as an orchestral score: *wind, rustling leaves, barking dogs, distant traffic, neighbours' voices, birdsong ...*

My black lab, Tsinuk, was always at my feet. When I wrote for too long she'd bring me my shoes in an attempt to lure me out for a walk, and if I ignored her for long she'd litter the hallway with every pair of shoes I owned.

She was good for me, Tsinuk.

We lived in the forest surrounding the village of Bear River, in southwest Nova Scotia. Our cabin was heated with a wood stove that I could also cook on. Winter power outages were no real concern, as the perishables could be packed in snow.

When Tsinuk did get me out walking we'd pass abandoned homesteads dating to the back-to-land movement of the late sixties and early seventies. Tsinuk adored rooting around these places for traces of olfactory history, but the scent of patchouli and musk were long gone and there was no longer anyone exhorting us to "get together and love one another right now."

Poet John Wall Barger had been there:

> It was 1975, I was five, and we'd just moved from southern California to a forest in Canada. First we lived in a tipi my mother stitched. I remember thinking it was odd that ferns were growing in the living room. My dad built a cabin out of an old house he helped tear down. I liked it in Bear River. I climbed and fell out of a lot of trees, and the deep eerie silence of those woods stuck with me.
>
> — John Wall Barger, interview 2010

Living old timey

There was another past here, still older than the counterculture's homesteading movement. These older farms had long dissolved into the earth, but occasionally I'd see lilacs blooming among the bracken and thorn and know that some turn-of-the-century farm wife had borrowed a cutting from a friend in town and planted it in an effort to make her dooryard a little more welcoming. And now here was this lilac tree, every May proclaiming that at one time the door and the farmwife had been very real.

Another living relic of these bygone days was a kind of music that called itself "bluegrass," "old time," or just "good music." It remains today a living proof of "them that's gone before."

Nova Scotia had been only one resting place for "the great Celtic diaspora" as comedian Ron James put it, but the music that could be directly linked to Scotland was found in Cape Breton Island, mostly. Southwest Nova Scotia, on the other hand, is more Irish and French influenced, the northernmost reach of Appalachian culture, not an appendage but a living part of the tradition, having contributed songs, singers, and new arrangements as the phenomena known as "country music" grew more popular.

There are many correspondences between Canada's Maritime Provinces and America's deep south: a similar mix of ethnicities (English, Scottish, Irish, French, African American, and Native American), the same economic woes, beautiful scenery, musical traditions, and a condescension bestowed on it from the rest of the country. Even the accents from some parts of the province sound Appalachian. (When Wilf Carter and Hank Snow, both from the province's south shore, went to Nashville most Americans, based on how they talked, assumed they were southern born and bred.[7])

But while country music south of the border was becoming an ever shinier commercial construct, rural Nova Scotians were still playing and writing new songs in the same old I, IV, V, I chord progression, using guitars, banjos, fiddles, spoons, autoharps, harmonicas, mandolins, and box drums. Sure, they were fans of the country singers they heard on the radio – they bought the records and watched the television specials – but it wasn't *their* music. It was too "classy," as I heard one man say, meaning that it was too polished, sounding closer to pop music than to the music sung at home.

Some of this music was homegrown (I didn't meet many musicians who didn't write at least some of their own material), but much of it came from the British Isles, Northern France, and Africa. The most popular southern artists were The Carter Family, their simple chord progressions and sentimental themes nearly at one with the homegrown country music of the Maritime Provinces.

An influx of Americans and Britons in the sixties and seventies and later meant that Nova Scotians became at least as musically sophisticated as anyone anywhere. But even in the midst of the folk festivals, classical performances, and indie experiments you could still find a core of music true to its origins.

Distilling old timey

Many of the younger generation, not just in Nova Scotia but in all of Appalachia and beyond, have been drawn to this magic and yearned to trap it, keep it alive, and bring out the crystalline beauty of its essence, a beauty that shines under the maudlin sentiment, repetitious chord structures, and monotonous instrumentation.

---

7 Schneider, Jason, *Whispering Pines: The Northern Roots of American Music from Hank Snow to the Band*, 2009 ECW Press

By the nineties this yearning had formed a strong movement revisiting the music of the past and seeking its core, kind of like what Tsinuk used to do around the old homesteads, rooting out the weird objects (clay inkwells, mechanical egg beaters, an old sabot) that had survived the transient ones (ink, eggs, feet).

> Old-time music is pre-bluegrass string band music. The music has more of a social purpose, for dances and for people to get together and play music and have fun. It's sort of an oral tradition of music. Bluegrass is obviously more performance-oriented. But there are very similar songs and repertoire between the two.
> — Jonathan Byrd, interview 2009

A missing link

My soundquest carried with it a stubborn curiosity as to what music had sounded like before being taken over by sound technology. I'd certainly never thought that sound technology diminished music, but I wanted to hear the old music in order to try to determine the difference, if any, that technology had made.

By the year 2000 I'd witnessed the passing of all those loved ones within whose childhoods all the music had been live as opposed to piped in. My maternal grandmother, born in Arkansas, had spent her early childhood in log cabins and sod huts without electricity. A flapper sensation at the local dance hall, she'd heard plenty of live music as a young girl, music from the gay nineties like "Buffalo Gals" and "The Band Played On," as well as minstrel show and Tin Pan Alley tunes. I regret never having asked her to try to remember for me the earliest songs of her childhood.

Where was I to find music that I could link to a past that had never been recorded?

Hymns

As my soundquest kept me picking through the flotsam and jetsam of my own history for voices of the distant past, I finally acknowledged that such voices been beside me all along.

There was only one kind of music that had remained fairly static for hundreds of years and longer, a genre regularly sung live in much the same way from the beginning: hymns.

Catholics and Protestants have long shared a body of songs carefully curated over hundreds of years of congregational singing, a sweet form of public music that has always included singers who are tone deaf, singers who warble off-key, singers who slide up to and down from high notes, singers who don't seem to know when to come in or fade out, and pianos just a little out of tune.

During my teen years every summer meant a visit to Harbinger, the Christian campground built by my paternal grandfather in the White Mountains. Rural New Hampshire too was part of Appalachia, not just geographically but culturally. When I saw the film *Oh Brother Where Art Thou* I knew the directors had understood the American musical roots landscape like the backs of their hands: I recognized those gospel-singing families, all dressed alike, the wailing high lonesome voices, the uncompromising mindsets.

The congregational singing in the chapel was enlivened by the musicians who filled the front rows. They played tambourines, guitars, fiddles, spoons, autoharps, and ukuleles, and there was even a trumpet player who'd once marched in Dixieland bands in New Orleans. Their sweet cacophony of praise was a clear demonstration of a holiness somewhere, a holiness that could be interpreted in many ways, misunderstood, even raged against, but never dismissed.

Hymns have provided priceless sustenance through generations of tribulation, and they may be the only living reminder we have of the music of our distant ancestors.

The oldest notated music found so far are hymns: the "Hurrian Songs," a 1400 BC collection of hymns carved in cuneiform on clay tablets, excavated in Northern Syria. Thanks to the wonders of information technology, you can actually listen to a performance of this music online. It's a strange thrill to hear such old music, music intended for praise and worship, brought to life, and to search it for music elements still in use today.

My alone times were often comprised of me, my guitar, and an old hymn book, singing "How Firm a Foundation," "It is Well With My

Soul," "Come Thou Fount," and "Oh, Love That Will Not Let Go." They kept my chin up through the rough stuff.

> Oh, Joy that seeks me through the pain,
> I cannot close my heart to Thee.
> I trace the rainbow through the rain
> And feel the promise is not in vain
> That morn shall tearless be.
> — From "Oh Love That Will Not Let Me Go,"
> by George Matheson, 1842-1906

On my last trip home I attended the Cherry Carnival Hymn Sing in Bear River. This had, when I lived there, been one of the highlights of my social calendar, despite its always being excruciatingly hot and plagued with technical issues. At this hymn sing Catholics and Protestants, rich and poor, black, white, and Mi'kmaq, all joined together to praise their creator, and even the faithless were moved.

Hymns are an unbreakable link with ancestors who suffered through things we can't imagine, who climbed mountains to carve decent lives out of nothing. And here their sacred songs were still alive with us in the new millennium.

Like everything else, this music was continuously transforming, yet somehow remaining the same.

Did I get an answer to my question about whether music had changed in response to technology? Maybe. The most salient difference seems to be that with technology music became more about exceptionality than communality. Hymns are a communal expression of worship; there are few stars, few memorable performances, and little hubris — that's not what hymns are about. Of course there were lauded composers, singers, and musicians before the invention of the phonograph, but without said phonograph the idolatry expended on their behalf was greatly limited.

My father once met a man who'd been Elvis Presley's Sunday School teacher and who described the young Elvis as sullen, difficult, and a lousy singer. For me this story sums up the relationship between religion and the entertainment world: The church supports a measure of artistry, but it hasn't much room for artists.

The task of artists in the secular age is to resist the inflation of the commerce-fed ego, at the same time asserting their value as creators. I've witnessed several musical careers in which I can see that this has been achieved. I am, however, completely at a loss as to how to describe exactly how they managed it.

The "alt" world

I can't remember when the "alt" (for "alternative") prefix first started appearing, but I know that by the early 2000s it was definitely a thing. There was alt-country, alt-rock, alt-folk, alt-jazz, even alt-punk (which sounded a little redundant). Three other prefixes appearing at roughly the same time were "indie," a term that seemed to refer more to means of production and distribution than to the originality of the work produced, "neo," suggesting a harking back to a genre that had faded from popular attention, and "post"– post-rock, post-classical, etc. "Post-" any genre suggested that the zenith of that genre's development had passed and that what we were now hearing was a rethinking of the musical tradition.

The alt, post, neo, and indie subgenres were evidence that artists were more interested in re-exploring bygone music than they were in creating new genres or continuing to develop existing ones. Who could blame them? With all the listening choices so readily available it was nearly impossible to create anything markedly different from what had come before. Besides, youth culture being something that had followed the early rockers into old age, there was no more generation gap, thus no need for music that rattled the grownups. The grownups had become unrattleable.

Composers and musicians were rather choosing to render existing musical genres more punk, more postmodern, more subversive, and more intense, thus making them their own while keeping traditions vibrant. Young musicians were hearing things in the past that spoke to them of themselves. It was like they were saying, "we're just like the past, only more so, and that's what makes us different."

Of all these movements the one that most attracted me was alt-country, at once an honouring of and a reaction to commercial country music.

The 2003 documentary film *Searching for the Wrong-eyed Jesus*[8] showed how the development of white southern music had been inextricably bound up in a spiritual vision, some of that vision coming out in religion that made no sense but which generated a powerful creative stimulus. As Jim White says of the preachers, teachers, and snake-handling Baptists he filmed, "It's so wrong it's right." There was a beauty in this music that defied aesthetic principles, and a meaning that confounded reason.

When I interviewed Rennie Sparks of The Handsome Family, a musical couple that appeared in the film, she expressed mild resentment at the director's efforts to get her to see herself in the context of a religiosity that wasn't hers.

"We had mixed emotions," she told me. "I'm not from the South nor am I Christian, so I was slightly annoyed at their insistence that my writing comes out of a Southern tradition. I grew up on Long Island in a very rural area. Very wooded and isolated, and I was always terrified at night."

Yet her writing, clearly inspired by Southern music, throbs with a keen sense of a spiritual presence. It was one of the many clues that it's in the nature of music, like it or not, to speak of other realities.

> No, no one hears the singing bones
> And no one sees the crying ghosts
> And everyone thinks I'm alone
> All alone.
> —The Handsome Family, "24-Hour Store"

The film created in me an obsession with Faulknerian lyrics, weirdly-tuned five-string banjos, and high, lonesome sounds. I began seeking out the hokiest old country recordings and the strangest "new" old country music I could find. I thrilled to the sounds of Lucinda Williams, Reverend Peyton, the Ebony Hillbillies, and the Carolina Chocolate Drops while buying up old albums by Hank Snow, Patsy Cline, and Johnny Cash at local yard sales. My alt-country soundquest slowly shifted gears with Sam Baker, who, although he had a rural sound, refused to call himself "alt" anything, or *anything* anything. One of the wonderful things

---

8   http://www.searchingforthewrongeyedjesus.com

about being a singer-songwriter is that you don't need a genre because you're basically a genre unto yourself, and Sam was even less definable than most. Sam's songs were to awaken me to some hard realities of our times and to the power of music to help us accept them while becoming neither paralyzed nor radicalized. Even better, he was the first artist I'd met who'd successfully resisted becoming a commercial idol while guarding and nurturing his unique gift to the world.

But more about Sam later. For now let's go into the ways in which musical artists were resisting.

New ways to make it in music

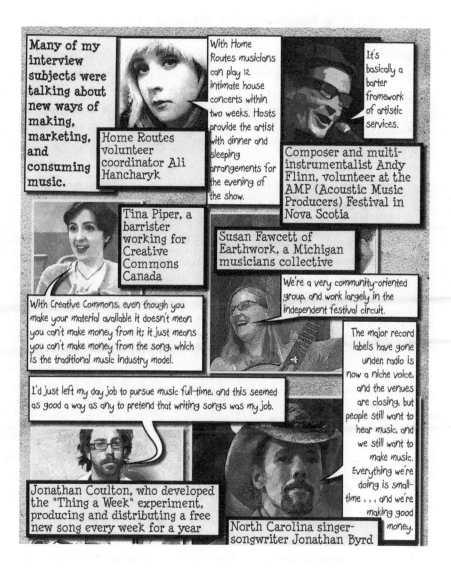

Many of my interview subjects were talking about new ways of making, marketing, and consuming music.

With Home Routes musicians can play 12 intimate house concerts within two weeks. Hosts provide the artist with dinner and sleeping arrangements for the evening of the show.

Home Routes volunteer coordinator Ali Hancharyk

It's basically a barter framework of artistic services.

Composer and multi-instrumentalist Andy Flinn, volunteer at the AMP (Acoustic Music Producers) Festival in Nova Scotia

Tina Piper, a barrister working for Creative Commons Canada

Susan Fawcett of Earthwork, a Michigan musicians collective

With Creative Commons, even though you make your material available it doesn't mean you can't make money from it; it just means you can't make money from the song, which is the traditional music industry model.

We're a very community-oriented group, and work largely in the independent festival circuit.

I'd just left my day job to pursue music full-time, and this seemed as good a way as any to pretend that writing songs was my job.

The major record labels have gone under, radio is now a niche voice, and the venues are closing, but people still want to hear music, and we still want to make music. Everything we're doing is small-time . . . and we're making good money.

Jonathan Coulton, who developed the "Thing a Week" experiment, producing and distributing a free new song every week for a year

North Carolina singer-songwriter Jonathan Byrd

Bucking the system – all over the planet

For reasons that should now be obvious, 2000 ushered in a trend toward developing new kinds of musical careers without the aid of corporations. Legal systems were being surprisingly accommodating, even contributing to the exploration of new funding models.

Creative Commons, an international movement to free up access to creative work, provides artists with alternative copyright arrangements. Creative Commons licenses have been drafted by several countries to help artists declare the specific rights they're granting along with the release of their work. When I asked Tina Piper, a barrister with Creative Commons Canada, how such an arrangement might help an artist make money, she had this to say:

> With Creative Commons even though you make your material available it doesn't mean you can't make money from it; it just means you can't make money from the song, which is the traditional music industry model. It doesn't mean you won't make money off of other parallel uses like merchandise or access to a website or any other of a number of things.
>
> Part of the idea behind Creative Commons is that the traditional model of copyright has been based on transferring the sharing of "the thing," the thing being the music, the poems, the song, the photograph, etc. We started to think that maybe it's not "the thing" that people want to pay for, but the experience. The other thing we found is that even if something is made freely available it's not that people don't want to pay for it. So you can make something available under Creative Commons and then under the terms of a pay-as-you-will kind of license if you want.
>
> — Tina Piper, barrister with Creative
> Commons Canada, interview 2009

In addition to pursuing alternative forms of licensing and monetizing, musicians were now developing more cooperative ways of helping advance each other's careers. In Nova Scotia in the early 2000s the musical duo Andy Flinn and Ariana Nasr helped organize a popular venue called Night Kitchen that proved a huge boon to DIY entertainers in the area. They rented the Al Whittle Theatre in Wolfville every few months to put on a variety show, charging $10 ($5 for those who didn't earn a regular salary) a head and splitting the proceeds among the performers. It was a great way for artists to get exposure and some grocery money.

Later on the same couple helped put together the AMP Festival, an initiative similar to Night Kitchen but more intensive and long term. Says Andy:

> We've talked to artists who came, say, from Montreal, with grant money to play at festivals here, and they've said, 'Yeah, we were paid two thousand dollars to get here and we spent seventeen hundred on the flight. Then there were other expenses.' So the military-industrial complex ended up with 80 percent of the grant money for the festival and the artist only got five percent.
>
> So right now we're working on the AMP (Acoustic Music Producers) Festival. Basically it's a Night Kitchen on steroids. It has the same pay scheme as Night Kitchen except all performers are recorded on a digital 8-track, shot with multiple cameras.
>
> We favour local artists in that we don't pay for travel. Your own community is the most stable network in your life. If somebody is in that phase of their lives when they wander and happen to pass by, then we're likely to be very welcoming, but we probably won't accept the financial burden of Air Canada shipping them from there to here.
>
> At the AMP Festival everyone has to play original music, because that's not legally encumbered, and all performers sign a release form to allow all the professional photographers to use the pictures any way they want.
>
> Also, the photographers sign a release allowing the performers to use their photos for CD covers, etc., without paying. And the performers don't have to pay a sound engineer to record them. It's basically a barter framework of artistic services.
>
> It's like creative commons, only event-bound. It's only one event, but unions form: a photographers union, a musicians union, an entertainment-staff-and-door-people union, and they all sign up for an AMP accord. With this you can now upload stuff to YouTube that is 100 per cent legally publishable.

Another case in point is Michigan's Earthwork Music collective, which proudly proclaims this mission statement: "The Earthwork Music collective believes in the intrinsic and historical power of music (and the arts) to raise both community and self-awareness."

> Earthwork Music is a collective of musicians, and we do a lot of benefit concerts and organize a few annual events, namely The Family Weekend (we offer classes for kids and their parents in the arts and sustainability), and the Water Festival a travelling music festival geared toward education. We are a very community-oriented group, and work largely in the independent festival circuit.
> — Susan Fawcett, interview 2007

In Saskatchewan the band Library Voices was using a collective called Young Soul Records to release all their recordings, trading musical resources with their colleagues on the label. The band's vocalist, guitarist, keyboardist, and lyricist, Michael Dawson, explained:

> The music industry has become a little too competitive; there's only so many shows and so many bands, so it becomes an issue of bands trying to get ahead of each other. That's not really the case here. A bunch of people are having records coming out in the collective and we appear on a bunch of those records and those musicians will be appearing on our full-length CD.
> — Michael Dawson, Library Voices, interview 2008

Jonathan Byrd happily extolled the virtues of the new career models:

> Everything we're doing is small-time: small venues, getting the word out though email or word of mouth, and we're making good money. The major record labels have gone under, radio is now a niche voice, and the venues are closing, but people still want to hear music and we still want to make music, and so there will always be a small-time. Music is coming back to people's parlours.
> — Jonathan Byrd, interview 2009

A great number of clever minds were recruited in the wake of this widespread rejection of those conventional machinations that had rarely aided real cultural development. Musicians themselves were coming up with means by which they could make at least a modest living, opposing a system in which a chosen few got all the golden stars and the rest went to rot.

And it was happening all over the world.

Nour Eldin Nageh Ali

In 2012, a year after the Arab Spring hit Egypt, I spoke with Nour Eldin Nageh Ali, composer and vocalist for Lel Wa Ain, a Cairo-based underground band.

"When the revolution came," said Ali, it actually gave us more opportunities, even television exposure. It was an amazing experience for me, the first time I sang before millions of viewers – something I had only dreamed of."

He pointed out that musicians' commitment to freedom was nothing new. Although media reports suggested that the revolution had changed the way musicians thought about music and encouraged alternative forms and political subjects, alternative forms, a love of freedom, and political lyrics had predated the revolution by decades and had probably fuelled the furor.

The difference now was that the audience for such music had expanded as media interest in alternative bands and performers had grown stronger. Those who wished to support home-grown music and creative freedom weren't weirdos and saboteurs anymore – they were influencers. There were fewer, if any, repercussions for singing openly about the need for justice and equality or for speaking truth to power.

The new Cairo music scene showcased local musical traditions that blend in foreign genres. One example is *mahragan* ("festival music"), which is also called electro-sha'bi. *Sha'bi* (or *chaabi*) originated in Algeria and developed distinct traditions all over North Africa. With its hard, driving rhythms and ecstatic and loud delivery, it's popular at weddings,. This tradition is always in flux, and international elements are constantly being added to it, lending it vibrancy and relevance.

The new music horizon is no bed of roses in Egypt. There's still uncertainty and a lack of resources along with the perennial temptation to sell out. Worse, there's no music education in public schools. There's also a lack of infrastructure to support alternative music. But judging by the ingenuity demonstrated by dedicated music activists, this is all changing.

Prior to the "Day of Rage" Ali had fought long and hard to make a niche for himself in the commercial recording industry, composing songs for big music studios. But when one studio wouldn't pay him for some of his material that they'd recorded, he began moving in a new direction, seeking out likeminded artists. In the beginning it wasn't easy to persuade good musicians to take a big risk and strike out on their own.

"My start was actually in 2008," remembers Ali. "I started my band with an oud player and drums. I tried to recruit other musicians, but everyone wanted a big record contract. I waited for around three years to make the band I have now. Like the other independent bands, we had to build a base of supporters for our music."

Ali's disappointment with the music industry paved the way for his acceptance of new music business models. Just as in North American folk music circles we see ingenious ideas being implemented to replace the traditional recording contract, so also the Egyptian music world is learning how to support alternative music. This allows the proceeds of CD and ticket sales to remain largely in the pockets of the musicians themselves.

"I don't think Egyptian music changed in response to the revolution," said Nour, "but more ordinary people started listening to underground music."

Lel Wa Ain, like other independent groups grown accustomed to poverty and anonymity, now found themselves the happy recipients of media coverage and an upsurge of gig requests. A fan base grew quickly from among native Egyptians and the foreigners who lived among them. But the infrastructure for the growth of this sector of the music industry wasn't there, and without it independent music remained clandestine.

Conventional models of music creation and promotion were designed to pipe more and more money to the upper turrets of the music industry and less and less to musicians. Record companies were willing to create only as many superstars as was necessary to make a music career seem attractive. This obliged up-and-coming artists to give over too much career control to the enterprise.

But in Cairo several independent entertainers decided to extend their maverick approach from making music to making a living on their own terms. As Nageh Ali explained:

> There's a great guitar player in Cairo now called Ousso. He has a diploma in guitar from America and he plays in Eftekasat, the most incredible jazz band in Cairo. Ousso had a unique idea that ended up being good for all of us. His idea was to have an underground concert. He came up with a really good business model to make this happen. It was called the S.O.S. Music Festival. Because of it, the underground bands in Cairo got more famous. The musician takes 50 percent of the money.

Since 2006 the annual SOS Music Festival has been providing free admission to audiences of 15,000 for eight hours of acts carefully chosen for their willingness to keep it real. Because the musicians are there to promote themselves and each other they share resources like equipment, technical skills, and services. Homegrown acts play alongside bands from other Middle Eastern countries, and North American genres are right up there with raï and chaabi.

"I love our Egyptian music," said Nageh Ali, "[but] I also love Western genres like jazz, blues, and reggae. I like to blend them together and I also like to find ways to mix all of these with Oriental and Sufi music."

There's a dimension of social concern in the band's lyrics and personal beliefs, but this comes across as difficult and hard-won, born of a determined struggle within the school of hard knocks.

> There's a tradition of songs here in Egypt that talk about fighting, corruption, politics, dictatorship, and democracy. When I was a child these kinds of songs were very important. There's one singer who's really famous for this kind of song – Mohamed Mounir.
>
> Mounir also developed a new musical genre in Egypt by mixing African with Oriental music and introducing elements of blues and hard rock, local music, [and] jazz.
>
> He talked about deep subjects, not like in commercial music. He motivated the people to be alive again, to move against the old regime.

The government tried to stop him from singing. He was outside of Egypt for a while. He wasn't exiled, but the government was really angry with him so he left for his own safety. He's a very cultured person, with great knowledge. And he cares about people; he gives concerts for a cheap price.

It was sobering to learn that recently the SOS Music Festival has succumbed to red tape and soaring costs. Here's hoping other models will rise to replace it.

DIY

What I'm really excited about is the increasing affordability of recording technology and the democratization of that process. It's incredible to be able to make records without being signed to a label.

The total budget for this EP, including the studio time, mix and mastering, and physical copies, was under $500. I have a recording setup that would have been absolutely out of reach financially to me a generation ago.

— Jesse French of the band King of Nowhere, interview 2017

In 2000 successful DIY albums weren't unheard of; it had been three years since Kathleen Hanna had closed her bedroom door to write and record all the parts for her cult smash album, *Julie Ruin,* on a multi-track recorder. Hanna, long-time girl-band vocalist and avid feminist team player, had managed to plan and produce a marketable and culturally relevant product all on her lonesome.

Kathleen Hanna could achieve this as early as the nineties because by this time she had plenty of experience as a performer and recording artist and could purchase the tools necessary to make her project succeed. The cost of even the most basic analogue recording equipment back then was more than your average student, burger flipper, or ne'er-do-well could afford, and only those who'd had some financial success could afford to indulge their personal creativity. Before the digital explosion most debutant musicians could afford neither studio time nor home recording equipment. In 2000 the dream was a lot closer, just not within easy reach. The belief was still widespread that the only way to make an album was to rent studio space and pay a professional. This is still a common misconception, but luckily so many pioneers have gone ahead that this prejudice is becoming a thing of the past.

My maternal grandfather used to delight us by reciting this verse from Edgar Guest:

> Somebody said that it couldn't be done
> > But he with a chuckle replied
> That 'maybe it couldn't,' but he would be one
> > Who wouldn't say so till he'd tried.
> So he buckled right in with the trace of a grin
> > On his face. If he worried he hid it.
> He started to sing as he tackled the thing
> > That couldn't be done, and he did it![9]

The fact that manufacturers scrambled to produce cheap tools for home recording owes as much to the courage of trail blazers like Hanna as it does to technology; before an industry moves in a new direction there has to be at least one person plowing ahead and doing what everyone says can't be done.

In the early years of the new millennium many music makers owned personal computers, and a market was opening up for digital audio work stations. Sure, musicians still had to pay for microphones, audio interfaces, external hard drives, and a host of other minor expenses, but the software for recording, mixing, and mastering sound recordings cost a fraction of the price of analog devices.

It would be another five years before Garageband would be released, enabling amateur creators to put tracks together by themselves. All they needed was time, something young people in the West generally had plenty of if they steeled themselves against social media's growing distractions. Garageband was so useful and user friendly that home-recorded Garageband songs were starting to appear in the top forty.

---

9   Edgar Albert Guest (1881-1859), "It Couldn't Be Done,"

The growth of desktop recording software also meant studio musicians could sell copyright-free sound samples and loops for home recordings, television, and radio.

What all this new software means is that much more music is being produced. We can wager that most of it is at least as bad as the pablum the record companies used to try to sell us. Sturgeon's law, which states that 90% of everything is crap, still holds true despite accessible software, or, perhaps, in part, because of it. You have to have fans in order to get that new album funded, so it's still tough to launch a career in music on your own.

Still, it's being done, thanks to the slowly dawning idea that you can ask for money. Before you get known the only people who'll be chipping in will be friends and family, but once you start growing your fan base it's your followers who'll be putting forth the money to fund your pressings, tours, and publicity.

Although a few brave souls had already asked their fans to donate money to help them tour or record a new album, the year 2000 saw the emergence of the first crowdfunding platform, ArtistShare. Other platforms were born soon afterwards. The idea wasn't really to take off until the end of the decade, but when it did, the world was ready.

The internet had been one key to this enabling and redirecting of cash flow away from top dogs and toward music makers. But home recording and crowdfunding were only a small part of what digital technology offered music makers the world over.

Another significant advance it brought in was the power of human connection.

A Brazilian band, a Canadian home tour, and a cuica

In 2003 Catherine and I were both let go from the group home organization. Catherine got a job at a women's center, where she immediately set about doing a world of good. I decided to go back to school to study psychology so that one day I could do good, too.

This couldn't have happened without distance education.

I was still living in a log cabin in the woods, far from any university, and with no car, but I did have dial-up internet. Relocating to find work was impossible at the time. I decided to take the route of distance education, a true godsend to Canadians living in the hinterlands.

Distance education has been around for a long time, but it used to be called "correspondence," and learning materials sometimes had to be dropped off in remote regions by small planes. Thanks to the internet people of all ages the world over could now enjoy the benefits of a university education – minus the distracting parties and soul-destroying love affairs – from our desktops, almost anywhere.

While taking courses in psychology and industrial relations from Athabasca University, I started writing about music for *The Voice*, the university's student union webzine. In 2010, while looking for new music on the then hip *MySpace*, I discovered Conjunto Roque Moreira.[10]

This couldn't have happened before social media.

The band blew me away with its potent vibe, multiple instruments, clever lyrics, manic stage performances, and passionate social concern. I quickly got in touch to request a CD and an interview.

This couldn't have happened without Google Translate.

---

10 https://myspace.com/conjuntoroquemoreira

Conjunto and I struggled to communicate. Anderson Almeida, the guitarist, could speak only a little English, and I spoke no Portuguese. I turned to *Google Translate*, an online tool that's been enabling people to confidently make fools of themselves in other languages since 2006.

I emailed them a bunch of questions. They emailed me their answers and snail-mailed me their self-produced debut CD. (A few years later they would have sent me a link to their album, but we weren't there yet.)

This couldn't have happened without digital recording technology.

In the 2013 film *Warm Bodies* a zombie who calls himself "R" has rescued his dream girl, Julie, and brought her to his lair inside a large abandoned airplane. The following conversation ensues:

> JULIE: What's with all the vinyl? Couldn't figure out how to use an iPod?
> R: Better . . . s-sound —
> JULIE: Oh, you're a purist, huh?
> R: — more . . . alive.

This scene plays out a discussion people have been having since the advent of compact discs, and it's more than a little droll that in this scene it's a zombie who's describing the sound of vinyl as "more alive."

With the compact disc we music lovers were sold a bill of goods. We were told the discs couldn't be scratched. Pshaw. We were sold expensive players that skipped and often just stopped playing. The worst of it was the deadness of the sound. We now know that the only digital sound formats that can approach the fullness of analogue sound are in un-compressed formats like aiff. But we weren't sold music in aiff; we were sold music in the compressed mp3 format, which accounted for why the music that had once thrilled us now sounded dull no matter how many tracks were piled on top of each other struggling to breathe or how many gimmicks the sound engineers had pulled off. And we were charged more than we'd been paying for our vinyl and cassettes, this for a tiny frisbee in an unwieldy plastic case housing graphics and text too small to see. Despite all that, the compact disc was a giant step forward.

I'll always be a flag-waving vinyl zealot, but to be fair, the audio world we inhabited before CDs was not an enviable one. For one thing, stereos had just kept getting bigger, better, and less affordable. We'd moved from those little suitcase phonographs to walls of throbbing sound.

If you paid less than a thousand bucks for your system you weren't a true music lover. Stereo snobs made the rest of us feel dirty. Magazines were filled with articles about which components to buy, and we were often reminded that a stereo only sounded as good as its weakest component.

All this began to change with the Sony Walkman, a tiny cassette player with a remarkably good sound, reasonably priced, that allowed you to take your music with you everywhere. Then there were ghetto blasters, a portable stereo you could load up with batteries and take to the nearest parking lot to party with your friends or use to accompany your breakdancing at the bus station. The prevailing opinion had changed; true music lovers didn't sell the farm for a fancy stereo — they took their music with them.

This mindset paved the way for the acceptance of digital technology; it might have begun with the purchase of a physical object, but it wouldn't be long before everyone was buying music in a form lighter than air: the mp3 file, downloadable from the internet and portable enough that thousands could fit on one mobile device.

Best of all, digital recording technology was a huge boon to indie artists, providing a means of creating and distributing recordings without recording contracts.

Those who wanted to produce and distribute their own music could now do so on the cheap, without having first achieved staggering popularity or impressed musically challenged CEOs. They could record their music on their home computers, where they could also burn CDs. Computer printers allowed them to create their own album covers, and the plastic cases could be bought at the local dollar store. The product could move straight from desktop to listener. Eventually there was no need for the disc at all, and many bands began creating "digital albums," available only in download form. It was a small window of opportunity, but it was opportunity nonetheless, and it was available to anyone who could get their hands on a computer.

But back to Conjunto . . .

In the 1970s in the state of Piauí in northeastern Brazil there lived a disc jockey named Roque Moreira whose whim it had been to only play the "B" sides of 45 records. The practice was a covert statement about the value of *all* an artist's work, not just the songs the record company picked. Moreira's radio show also formed a kind of early social media network, broadcasting listeners' messages to each other across the region.

His show left a lasting mark on a group of teens from Teresina who were later to form the band Conjunto Roque Moreira (the "Roque Moreira Band"). Naming themselves after the DJ had been dictated by their fans, who, on hearing Conjunto's boisterous, danceable, genre-blending tunes, had quickly associated them with the maverick DJ.

A stew of musical influences

Conjunto Roque Moreira's music is a rich mix of genres – *baião, xote,* samba, reggae, classical Indian, *embolada, repente,* bossa nova, blues, jazz, rhythm and blues, funk, acid rock, British prog rock, rhythm and blues, and '60s folk anthems, to name just a few.

> Like people, all rhythms have something in common. There may be several meanings for a word, just as there can be several words for one meaning. Music is characterized by accents, and this is hard to feel or translate, but it's by experiencing that we reach the right spot. Our role is to expand the variety of music in the world and to make our fans dance, uniting them in a love of life.
> —Anderson Almeida, Conjunto Roque Moreira, interview 2010

Singing out

The band wasn't so busy letting the good times roll that it didn't have time to speak out against social injustice. Their repertoire contained songs like "NoNoNo,"[11] exhorting citizens to scrutinize the actions of politicians before voting. "Vendedor de Cajuína" (Cajuína's Seller) is about the power of working people. "Magia Nordestina" (Northeast

---

11 https://www.palcomp3.com/conjuntoroquemoreira/nonono

Magic) speaks of the hardships of the peoples in Brazil's arid regions. And "Velho Monge" (Old Monk) talks about the river in Teresina and its importance to the fisher people who live there.

The members of Conjunto Roque Moreira taught themselves to make *darbukas, djembes, caxixis, berimbaus, cuícas, gopyangs,* drumsticks, *carinhões,* and *contrabaldes,* all from a mix of organic and recycled materials, sometimes copying existing instruments and sometimes designing their own.

"Some of our instruments are traditional, from Brazil," said Almeida, "and others are from Africa, because of the great influence that Brazilian music has received from African music."

Conjunto Roque Moreira – the Canadian tour

After I published a review and an interview with the band online, they asked me if I could help them get a tour in Canada. It happened that I'd just interviewed Jonathan Byrd, the folksinger from North Carolina, who'd introduced me to a new Canadian touring model that was enabling indie musicians to make a living.

Curious, I got in touch with one of these newfangled organizations, Home Routes (*Chemin Chez Nous*). This lead to an interview with volunteer coordinator Ali Hancharyk, who explained how the system worked. Home Routes would select suitable applicants and send them on a tour of homes in rural Canada. The hosts were volunteers who asked for no reward but the privilege of hosting musical artists. The hosts, who needed to have a performance space in their homes in order to qualify, would invite local people over to hear the performers play, charging $15 a head. The musicians got to keep every penny.

I broached the idea of a Home Routes tour to Almeida, who instantly took to it. I then sent an email to Home Routes recommending Conjunto Roque Moreira. At Almeida's request I emailed another letter of recommendation to the appropriate cultural department of the Brazilian government.

Frankly, I was doing it to be nice; knowing from experience the nightmare of red tape sometimes required to enter Canada, I expected it all to come to nothing.

But before I could say "border fascists" Conjunto was in Manitoba gladdening hearts in one house concert after another. Almeida sent me photos of the band members being happily embraced and applauded by passels of chortling Canadians.

Home Routes thanked me for recommending the band, saying that Conjunto had been a big hit in every home. Conjunto asked me to come to one of their concerts, as they had a thank-you gift for me. Unfortunately, I was three hours away by air. I gave them my heartiest congratulations and apologized for not having the wherewithal to make it to one of their performances.

They mailed me the gift. It was a *cuica*, which means "opossum" in Portuguese, so named because of the sound it makes. It looks like a drum but is played by rubbing a wet cloth up and down a wooden rod inside, making that adorable squeaky noise you hear in bossa nova and samba.

Roque's Factory: No ivory towers

Somewhere in the process of perfecting their designs and scouting out the best materials the band got the idea that they might be able to help out needy local kids by teaching them how to play these instruments and even how to make them. Thus was born *Fábrica do Roque* (Roque's Factory), a community-based project empowering the poor for creative expression, positive interdependence, and greater self-sufficiency.

It was the kind of naturally compassionate response musicians are capable of making once they get their egos out of the way and just let it happen. We won't find any ivory towers on the Conjunto Roque Moreira planet, nor art for art's sake, nor regressions into absinthe, isolation, and macabre ideation. Nor will we find a self-righteous and grim resolve to change the world at all costs. Instead the group manifests a robust and generous creativity that blossoms naturally into positive action while managing to stay fun. It was this band that opened my eyes to what artists could be and gave me a model to help me find subjects for my *Mindful Bard* column.

The musicians promote the use of organic and recycled materials in order to teach the young the importance of cherishing and preserving nature. They even use some of the child-crafted instruments in their own performances.

"Even in difficult times," said Almeida, "we can get enough inspiration to create, because crazy people believe in their dreams. It's in the need for innovation that creativity flourishes."

This glorious blend of art, compassion, and craziness could never have been realized except by people who remained physically and emotionally connected to their communities in a digital world. In Brazil music had always been a highly social give-and-take, the very hub of their childhood games, family gatherings, parties, dances, and stints in many bands. There was never a question of separating art from social engagement.

Parallels of this story were happening the world over as musicians grappled with maintaining their humanity in the midst of life's changing conditions. Those who won did so, as had Conjunto Roque Moreira, by jettisoning their egos, skirting the starmaker machinery, remembering their people, and seeking inventive ways to benefit from the new technologies.

The breaking of the kindest of hearts

In early November, 2018, a member of the group sent me a saddening message:

> This is an outburst of a Brazilian friend who is struggling to one day see his country free from fascism.
>
> On Sunday the 28th there was elected a new president; he has already begun to carry out various atrocities with the population, the environment, with the Indians, and with the poorest. His government authorizes people to use guns and to commit crimes against blacks, homosexuals from the Northeast, and the poor.
>
> We Brazilians are fighting against this fascist government because we know that if he is not stopped very innocent people will suffer a great barbarity.

He sent a video of an excavator ploughing into frail houses while poor families stood helplessly by. He explained:

> Here already are some actions after the elections, together with the police expropriating residents from their homes.
>
> In some cities, such as São Paulo, Rio de Janeiro, and Minas Gerais, the police are already authorized to kill regardless of the approaches taken by the people on the streets.
>
> Some Brazilian institutions will stop encouraging cultural activities and artistic expressions. Some media are being censored. One of the newspapers of great importance is being threatened with closure.
>
> We are living a mixture of insecurity and intolerance.

Brazil has long been a centre of cultural ingenuity, mostly in the realm of music, but also in literature and the other arts, leaving its mark on the world by influencing and inspiring artists everywhere. Most of this richness has been generated by the country's most oppressed ethnic minorities, just as happened in the United States.

Jazz singer Stacey Kent echoed these impressions in our interview in 2011:

> If I were to choose where my musical heart really lives, it's in Brazil. The Brazilian sensibility is something [my husband and I] totally relate to as people, not just as musicians. It's a country made up of different groups of misplaced peoples who ended up making a whole new culture. Something fascinating happened there. You can say the same thing about the United States. We can't romanticize it because there were often horrible circumstances. But in Brazil they sing about it. There's all this pain going on, so they sing, dance, and rejoice in the pure and simple joy of living.

Today we see another commonality between Brazil and the United States: both seem tangled up in the free rein given the lowest of characters.

Jair Bolsonaro, who assumed power on January 1st, 2019 as Brazil's 38th president, is a former army captain as well as a fan of military rule, a defender of torturers, openly supportive of dictatorship, and vocally and maliciously opposed to gays, blacks, and women. He claimed to be the country's one-way ticket out of corruption, recession, and crime and yet seems ready to set up all the conditions necessary to create hotbeds of lawlessness.

Everything I've learned about Brazil from Conjunto de Moreira assures me that this is simply the swinging of a pendulum. It will swing back. But in the meanwhile the spirit will grieve, and once more the beautiful, haunting music of broken hearts will rise to the clouds.

For those who remained grounded in their own humanity and in social concern the Internet has been a marvellous tool of personal and creative development, making it easier for musicians and music lovers from all over the world to connect and participate in each other's careers. It's made it easier to learn, to write, to be read, to communicate with people in other languages, to produce and disseminate one's own music, to spread liberal ideas, to institute social programs, to create new DIY models of music management, publicity, and distribution.

Unfortunately it has also fuelled the growth of populism, a major threat to personal freedom and thus to all artists.

Populism owes its existence in part to terrorist acts, which can be used to whip up fear and bigotry. Terrorism, populism's extreme, also aided and abetted by digital technology, can be blamed on a complex of historical and cultural factors, not least of which is the longstanding and wilful blindness of leaders to the plight of the poor.

Music in the time of terror

January, 2008: A memorable phone session with Texan singer-songwriter Sam Baker, who'd survived a terrorist attack in Peru in 1986

I'd been sitting with a German family on the train to Machu Picchu.

The parents couldn't speak English, but the boy could, and we struck up a conversation.

The bomb was in our train car.

When it went off it killed my friends and the German family—in a particularly terrible fashion.

I stayed alive in spite of subdural bleeding, cranial bleeding, gangrene, and renal failure.

You see quite a bit after weeks when you can't move, near death. It makes you reflective.

I try not to use a word like 'wrong,'
But I carry a torch.
It burns my hand.
I'd like to lay it down
In the Promised Land.
    –Sam Baker, "Angel Hair"

In 2015, after a terrorist bomb killed 17 foreign tourists at the Bardo Museum in Manouba, Tunisia, just walking distance from our apartment, my husband and I stopped at our favourite local café. As we sat down at an outside table everyone around us rose and left. I don't know if it was just a coincidence or if they really did think foreigners were no longer safe to be around.

In Tunisia I saw up close the social conditions best suited to incubating and releasing terrorism, conditions frighteningly similar to those growing more widespread in the West today: ignorance, poverty, hopelessness, social marginalization, harsh penal systems, a lack of social solidarity, and a conviction that the world can only be reformed by means of a religion or ideology forcibly imposed on a frightened populace.

To cripple with fear

The first 20 years of the new millennium have witnessed 9/11, the Istanbul explosions of 2003, the New Delhi and London bombings of 2005, and other attacks in Norway, Moscow, Madrid, and Mumbai, not to mention many smaller attacks worldwide, carried out by a range of terrorist groups with different motives but sharing the same goal: to enforce compliance by means of fear.

Terrorism has proven itself futile in the pursuit of all but the briefest of goal achievements, yet it still manages to persuade marginalized young people the world over to sacrifice their lives to kill and destroy in the name of dogmas and ideologies. Why are the young so often recruited to malicious organizations and dispatched to destructive plots? Think about it: In the throes of the hormonal tempests of adolescence none of us has ever been at our wisest.

In the first chapter I asked where our pied pipers were today. It appears that they're everywhere, but they're not making music. Many in fact see music as an evil to be stamped out. Like the pied piper in the story they feel cheated, and the recompense they demand is our children.

It's ever so much easier for them now. The technological changes that facilitated the making and experience of music in our time have also enabled terrorist organizations, making recruitment and logistics faster and cheaper. Converts are won before they know what hit them, leaving them later wondering at what point they should have turned back.

Puppet-masters and cannon fodder

As laid out in Ian Johnson's, *A Mosque in Munich: Nazis, the CIA, and the Rise of the Muslim Brotherhood in the West,* the Holocaust and Cold War puppet-masters didn't retire with the Allied victory: their legacy lived on in a series of little known political initiatives. These initiatives eventually supplied international terrorist groups with the same weapons, training methods, tactics, and even aggression-inducing drugs that the Nazis, the Stalinists, and the CIA used to train their predecessors in the service of global dominance.

Their brains have even been soaked, lathered, and rinsed in the same racist propaganda, and like their Nazi, Stalinist, and CIA predecessors, the new terrorists regard their followers as just so much cannon fodder.

In addition to aiding terrorists' organization and recruitment, digital technology and the Internet have rendered the experience of terror more effective and permanent. We don't just live in fear of unwanted surprises; when the living nightmares arrive we can watch them again and again on a host of screens.

Despite advances in technology and reams of research suggesting that trauma must be treated immediately, psychological services the world over have woefully failed to respond to rising rates of PTSD.

Might musical artists address all this pain and help us get back to the garden, if in fact there's a garden left? It's complicated, which is why we're looking at the story of one music maker who survived a terror attack, emerging with an awakened sense of what matters. For Sam Baker, the natural outcome of recovery was a musical output that transcended fear and despair.

Envisaging a world of acceptance

Sam Baker's cryptic lyrics are set to music so evocative of the open prairie that you can almost smell the sagebrush. His songs, slow, tender, bare, and reverent, grant a grittily serene vision of the saints and sinners of a Texan dreamscape, a rich microcosm of the world at large.

Baker's perspective and aesthetic changed completely while he was recovering from a train bombing carried out by Peru's Shining Path, a militant communist group. His terrible suffering granted him a deeper connection with humanity and a sense of the sacredness of the moment.

He's not the first American terror survivor, but he's certainly one of the most eloquent, his slow recovery coinciding with the burgeoning of a compassion that informs his songwriting. Baker moves past blame and bitterness to envisage a world wherein we awaken from the collective nightmare to accept and love each other in all our beauty and baseness. I've come to see this as essential to the spirit of music itself.

In an interview with Dan Forte for *Wood and Steel Magazine* Baker described what it was like being close to death for weeks, unable to move: "It was an interesting time. Very introspective. The only thing that came in loud enough to really get through that haze or fog or internal trauma I was dealing with was the raw suffering of others."

Sam's spiritual focus suggests one of the most rewarding but difficult of Zen disciplines – the importance of living in the now. He emerged from the darkness with treasures in his hands, not the least of which being an understanding of the futility of divisions:

> What if everything is perfect right now? By perfect I mean whole and complete, all you need available to you at this very moment. It doesn't mean you're not responsible for making things better. We should all be more responsible and more compassionate, but what if it's you in the face of God this second? You can then get outside of yourself. This whole thing where you and I are separate and look at ourselves as if we were players on a football field – we can get past that.

God is in every face we meet, and not just in every face – in every plank of cedar that's tacked onto the outside of our houses, in the rosemary that grows in the yard. The question then becomes: How can I learn not to turn away?

What I saw in that terrible thing in South America is that we're all essentially connected. There's an attitude that says, 'I'll wear this red hat or this white hat and because of that I have something that gives me access to a different spiritual realm.' I think our spiritual realms are right here with us all the time.

—Sam Baker, interview 2008

Sam Baker was a milestone in my career as a professional listener. But the subject of senseless violence wasn't done with me. An online encounter with Kurdish oud-player Mustafa Mallabozan at the start of the Syrian Civil War opened my eyes to truths almost too beautiful to acknowledge.

The kurd's tale

The Kurds are a fierce and tender folk living in Turkey, Iraq, Iran, and Syria.

In spring of 2010 the Kurds of Kobany, Syria, celebrated themselves. Mallabozan played bouzouki with his friends before a great happy crowd.

It was a glorious affirmation of Kurdish identity.

And it was illegal.

The next day the law was heavily enforced. After three months Mallabozan left prison with a shattered knee, having lost his hair and his mental health to torture, abuse, and malnutrition.

Apparently the voluntary music of a free people was a serious threat to power.

Sometimes paranoia's just having all the facts.
— William S. Burroughs

I first began texting with Mustafa Mallabozan, a Kurdish poet and musician from Kobany, Syria, in 2011, on a language-learning site. I've corresponded with him off and on since the civil war began, and since then he's lived in refugee camps and has traveled across Turkey, Iraq, and Lebanon.

I'd been using the site ostensibly to learn other languages but unofficially to gather narratives from people in strife-torn Middle Eastern countries. I wasn't eager to learn Kurdish, but I longed to hear first-person accounts of the Syrian war and to learn more about Middle Eastern musical genres. Mallabozan wanted to practice his English, so it looked like a win-win, but almost immediately we became embroiled in a series of minor spats due to language problems, cultural misunderstandings, and, as I learned much later, his very legitimate fear that our conversations were being monitored.

The first time I'd read about the Kurds was in *The Anabasis* (*The Retreat of the 10,000*), a 5th-century B.C. Greek history written by a certain General Xenophon. The Persian prince Cyrus the Younger had hired the Greek hoplites to aid him in his fight for the throne. Cyrus was killed just after the Greeks arrived in Persia, and so the Greeks, having come all that way, had to turn back around and return home, pursued by Cyrus's enemies, including the formidable Tissaphernes.

They couldn't return to Greece using the route they'd come, because they were 10,000 strong and had fed themselves by killing most of the wild game along the way. Their only choice was to take a rather circuitous and difficult path back through the mountains of what is now Kurdistan, Armenia, Iraq, and Turkey.

One of their many ordeals was fighting hostile mountain tribes, including the *Carduchoi*, the ancestors of present-day Kurds. Like the Greeks, the Carduchoi were the enemies of the Persians, but the villagers didn't know this when they spied the Greek army marching their way; they reacted with all the aggression they could muster, attacking the Greeks with slings and longbows:

"Seven days spent in traversing the country of the Carduchians had been one long continuous battle," wrote Xenophon, "which had cost them more suffering than the whole of their troubles at the hands of the king and Tissaphernes put together."

Xenophon had my sympathy. In my conversations with Mallabozan, I had to work very hard to be diplomatic in an effort to get clear answers to my questions. Part of the problem was his limited English, but he got irked by my requests for greater detail. He sometimes accused me of having no plan and of being ignorant of Syrian politics. At one point he asked me if I needed his help with English because I seemed to be having trouble understanding his.

Mallabozan's abrasiveness aside, İ admire the Kurds. Like the Irish, the Romanov gypsies, and the African Americans, their music and poetry throb with a deep knowledge of suffering that renders their longing for beauty especially poignant and their pugnacity forgivable. From the dawn of their history, the Kurds have been oppressed to varying degrees by whatever mega-power happened to be ruling their environs. This has not abated; their genocide by Saddam Hussein is now a matter of historical record, and in Syria they've been brutally targeted by the Assad regime.

To make things worse, the Kurds were now tangled up in a web of conflicting loyalties. Syria had at least ten Kurdish parties under the umbrella of the Kurdish National Council (KNC), a body working toward greater autonomy for Kurdish Syrians. In conflict with the KNC was the Partiya Karkerên Kurdistan (PKK), or Kurdistan Workers Party. The PKK was an international socialist Kurdish organization, based in Turkey, that provided protection against armed groups to Syrian Kurdish cities, including Mallabozan's Kobany. This was a little ironic considering that the PKK was almost universally believed to be a terrorist organization, having claimed credit for a number of kidnappings, hijackings, and armed assaults in Turkey, Northern Iraq, and Western Europe.

It was clear that Mallabozan and his community were extremely vulnerable — and that the bullets could come from any direction.

While Mallabozan remained in Syria every discussion with him started out congenially and ended by drowning in misunderstandings. To add to the frustration level, the power in Kobany was turned off several times a day at regular intervals to conserve electricity.

But one day he had something for me. He'd told me that his group, a band of intellectuals, artists, teachers, and professionals, would soon be in Kobany participating in a big demonstration they'd helped organize.

He promised me photos. Fabulous! I would write it up and sell the article to a major paper. I told him I'd need to talk to his friends as well. *No problem.*

I checked the news, and sure enough, a large demonstration transpired, exactly where he said it would and for the reasons he'd given me. I couldn't wait to talk to Mustafa again and to see his photos.

When a few days later I found him online he was agitated and confused. He'd been to the doctor but the doctor couldn't help him, he said. Nothing felt right. Even his scarf had betrayed him.

The disappointment was crushing: My "inside source" was clearly psychologically unstable, and I just didn't have a story. I wished him well and moved on.

Once I'd risen above the self-pity I asked myself if sanity had any place in Assad's Syria. Perhaps reason had been completely driven from the country and one could no longer witness what was happening except through a fog of paranoia. Even the normally sound of mind were experiencing the worst symptoms of post-traumatic stress disorder.

One of the purposes of both war and terrorism is to delegitimize suffering by rendering witnesses mentally incapable of testifying to their own experiences. In the Syrian civil war, gaslighting the masses has proven remarkably effective.

Another stint

Mallabozan had made one of his habitual visits to Lebanon, and when he returned to Syria via Homs his bus had been stopped by government forces. From his window he witnessed an incidence of brutality that he tried to record on his cellphone. He was seen, arrested, and imprisoned once more.

After his release, he contacted me again. Normally swaggering with bravado, Mustafa was now skittish. He couldn't sleep and was obviously drinking too much. He noted with agitation that an email message I'd sent him had been opened before he'd gotten to it. He still wanted to get his story out, but he insisted that from then on I contact him only on his Turkish cellphone number, the only one he felt was safe.

One day on Facebook I asked him about the PKK, and he began telling me what he knew. Suddenly his tone changed from warm to icy.

"Hey, you know I'm not so high educated," he wrote, "and I went to school just ten years. And what you asked is about policy and my work is in industry. I have had a factory. If you ask me about employment here in these countries I can answer you very well."

Not educated? Mustafa was multilingual and extremely well-read. Even if he had dropped out of school early, his autodidactic habits had effectively rendered him smarter than the average bear. And this was the first I'd heard of a factory.

I asked if I could talk with his friends, a privilege he'd proffered earlier, but now he was insisting that they were all simple, uneducated men like him (before he'd said they were writers and professionals). Then he asked me if I knew Bryan Adams, breaking into a strange code that I interpreted to mean I should talk to him tomorrow, that he would have something for me then.

It finally got through my thick skull that he was acting, sending me covert messages warning me against revealing anything to whomever might be spying on our conversation.

He later suggested that the trauma of war was taking its toll on mental health in Kobany. Was this true or still part of a code?

> Not just me have this illness – almost all of my friends have it. I think it's because of the weather. It's turned from winter to spring. Some of my friends don't sleep at home because of their illness. They had the same illness which I have now, but I'm still sleeping in my home, thank God. They are sleeping in hospital.
> — Mustafa Mallabozan, private email message 2012

Because of the *weather?* His country was getting bombed to dust. Others living in Syria kept asking, *Why doesn't America do anything?* From where I was standing, there was nothing America or anyone could do. *Get out,* I repeated again and again. *Just get out, and we'll do all we can to help you.*

The smell of a soul

Human beings are so made that the ones who do the crushing feel nothing; it is the person crushed who feels what is happening. Unless one has placed oneself on the side of the oppressed, to feel with them, one cannot understand.

—Simone Weil

I wrote to Mallabozan to warn him about some things in the article I was writing about him. I needed to know that sharing my opinion of his mental health wouldn't destroy our friendship. I also strongly suggested that for his safety I use an alias for him. His reply:

Thank-you if will write something about me, and please you can use my real name ... Never mind about me, never be worried about this, and please, I won't ask you to tell something you didn't find ... in me and in our conversations. If you think what ... you write about me is true and real, just do it. I won't ask you to describe me as an angel, as I'm not. If I will feel offended, I will thank you because you opened my mind about something I didn't know about ...

—Mustafa Mallabozan, private email message 2013

One day I received the following email:

Today, my cousin died as a martyr. He was [a] soldier, and my day was so busy and tired. He was 21 years old, just as a flourishing flower, an angel to all of us. Today so many strange things happened to me, without sleeping until noon today. They called us [to tell us that] he died and that his body was in Aleppo and would in some hours be in my city, Kobany.

In this time some of the young, we went to dig a grave. It's not the usual feeling, the usual sense. So strange, digging a hole and I know someone I loved will sleep in this hole. I was helping him, but in so sad a way. When he arrived he had been dead 20 days. There was such a strange smell from his body; I wondered at this smell. Was it body smell or soul smell?

—Mustafa Mallabozan, private email message 2013

His cousin had been killed while fighting with the same government forces that had imprisoned Mallabozan several times. He'd lost his life at the hands of the Free Syrian Army.

"But this does not mean that we are against the Free Syrian Army!" Mustafa insisted.

After burying his cousin, Mustafa wrote:

> All my religious thinking should be changed. I should pray, I shouldn't drink alcohol anymore. I have to be ready to meet my God any time. Happiness can be taken from us at any time – we don't know how. Death is close to us, and we have to be ready to be confident to meet our God and show our white book to the angels and to God.

A heart in love with beauty

> A heart in love with beauty never grows old.
> — Kurdish proverb

Back to July, 2012: Mallabozan is in Iraqi Kurdistan. He asks me if I'd like to see an Iraqi sunset. He pans his webcam around the refugee camp, saying in his slow, methodical English, "I suppose to you this is not so great, but to me it is really amazing."

I see a broad plain and a low mountain range, and yes, the sunset is lovely. A friend of his walks by, a fellow Kurd who lives with his wife and children in the same camp. Mallabozan introduces us. I play my guitar and sing "I Shall Not Be Moved" while they smile with delight.

The door to madness

> The courage of the poet is to keep ajar the door that leads into madness.
> — Christopher Morley

Mallabozan has a poet's nature; he not only exemplifies the poetic persona, he writes ecstatic, authentic, heartfelt poems. His door to madness is ajar.

Now that Mallabozan is living in Austria the paranoid tenor of his conversation has dissipated. Is this because the trauma of his last prison stay has weakened or because Assad's tentacles are loosening their hold on cyberspace? I have no way of knowing, but I'm glad to see him get his groove back.

I've already pointed out that one of the more tragic effects of violence is to silence the voice of suffering by rendering victims so deeply disturbed that they're no longer capable of faithfully relaying their suffering to the outside world. Now I wonder if violence can also silence music.

There are fundamentalist Christian groups who've forbidden music or at least restricted instrumentation (the violin, the bass, and the guitar have all held terms as "devil's" instruments). But for most of Christendom music is an integral part of worship. I've spoken with several conservative Muslims who insisted that music was forbidden according to their religion. They were irked when I pointed out that the calls to prayer and the manner in which the Quran is read are forms of music. Yet one can find music-filled worship, especially among the Sufi Muslims, and Sunnis and Shias gladly revel in music outside the mosque at home and at weddings. Strict communists and fascists insist that music, as all the arts, should serve the state, effectively restraining creativity. My opinion rests with Willie the Shake:

> The man that hath no music in himself,
> Nor is not moved with concord of sweet sounds,
> Is fit for treasons, stratagems, and spoils;
> The motions of his spirit are dull as night,
> And his affections dark as Erebus.
> Let no such man be trusted. Mark the music.
> —William Shakespeare in *Merchant of Venice*

The longer I live the more I'm certain that the music-hating charlatans posing as more righteous and patriotic than the rest of us are wolves in sheep's clothing, their "affections dark as Erebus," despite the mask of virtue.

"Kissing my instrument"

For Mallabozan music was a kind of religion unto itself, a warm splendor filling his heart with joy and uniting him with his family, his people, and all of humanity, alive and dead.

His first instrument was one he'd fashioned from a metal box and a wooden stick. As soon as he could afford "real" instruments he'd practiced for at least ten hours a day for three years, from 2006 to 2009, with no teacher. The rest of his free time was spent listening to music.

"Because of the big amount of happiness," he wrote, "I was just laughing loudly, kissing my instrument as if it was my life partner."

In a way, it was.

Music as language

Mallabozan continued:

> The music I listened to when I was younger, it was talking to me. For example, Muhammed Abdulkarim – a Syrian bouzouki player called the 'Prince of Bouzouki' – his playing used to speak to me. For years I would listen to his playing before I slept, and his playing was talking to me in real words, each musical phrase of the prince was a word sentence and someone telling it to me.
>
> I don't remember the last time I wanted to hear music. I prefer silence to notes. I enjoy it, really; it's maybe a kind of dead soul in a living body. But it's like this now.

How sad, that last remark. If Sam Baker's story showed that people are able to form significant, healing musical statements in the aftermath of devastating violence, Mallabozan's proved that the musical brain itself was somehow threatened by organized cruelty. It won't be easy for anyone to convince me now that terrorism and tyranny can't destroy music, because I've seen that for at least a little while they can.

The creator-slave

> For me creating music is like creating the world. It's strange to say, but for me when we create a new song we create a new environment, a new world, new meanings, something that we hope has never been done.
> —Jici LG, vocalist and guitarist
> for Mangeur de Rêves, interview 2019

I'd developed an intense curiosity regarding the music of the slave, the exile, the rejected, the refugee. It all begged the same question: *If oppression can silence music, why does the purest and most beautiful music nearly always begin with slaves?*

One day while reading "The Fisherman and the Flounder" to my little goddaughter I had an epiphany: The fisherman's wife wasn't punished for her greed and pride until she demanded to be "as God is," and her return to the pigsty wasn't the penalty for reaching too high. It was rather the precise granting of her wish.

She had asked to be as God is, and whatever God was had been in the pigsty all along.

The terrorism of our time forces us to question all our beliefs. It forces poets to become songwriters, distilling horror and beauty in fantastic combinations. It makes healing music urgent. God is in the pigsty. Sometimes you have to go there to hear him singing.

History of Gnawa

Gnawan musician, ca 1900 in Morocco

A guembri, the Gnawan stringed instrument with the droning bass string

Gnawan music was designed to induce trance states.

Acts like Aziz Sahmaoui & University of Gnawa keep the tradition vibrant.

The conditions of creative achievement

> I think we're about ready for a new feeling to enter music. I think
> that will come from the Arabic world.
> — Brian Eno

Remembering that jazz might not have been possible if not for the
unique social context of the Jim Crow years in the postwar south, one
can't help but wonder if the North African artists had some unique historical condition that explains their achievements in the third millennium.

Sure enough, such a condition exists. It's called "exile."

If there's any mercy in injustice it's that it sometimes creates fertile
soil for the explosion of genius. North African immigration to Europe
and North America enabled advanced genre-mixing, bringing indigenous genres to other countries and also making of that music a means
of uniting musicians around the world.

Why did so many North Africans leave their beloved homes? Why
did a people so attached to the hearth, to communal life, to family, pull
up roots and leave in such great numbers?

It's complicated, but by most accounts the most destabilizing influence in Muslim societies today is Islamic extremism, a dark force that
has undermined social orders, damaged economies, and created an
atmosphere of fear and despair from which moderates long to escape.

The magnetism of Morocco

I was first drawn to Moroccan music in 2009 while reading *The No-
Nonsense Guide to World Music,* by Louise Gray.[12] Gray chose a thoroughly
postmodern structure by building her book around the most moving,
intense, and influential musical genres the world over, genres I saw as
fountainheads of primal musical energy. The genres that stood out were
Spain's fado, Greece's rembetika, and the Sufi music played in the Dje-
maa el Fna marketplace in Marrakech, Morocco.

---

12 Gray, Louise, *The No-Nonsense Guide to World Music*, Between the Lines, in association
    with New Internationalist Publications Ltd., 2009

"Happy, man!"

Morocco had long been a relatively repressive country and in 2009 was becoming more so. Poverty, high youth unemployment, government corruption, and exasperating religious discipline were creating a stifling hopelessness. Moroccan blogger and poet A.T.B. summed up the Moroccan youth experience as a daily schedule of glorious escapes through American television – followed by rude awakenings:

> Happy, man!
> just happy!
> until we grudgingly shuffled outside
> to find the horizon had sucked
> the sun in leaving behind
> a smudge of colors like a
> fly swatted against the wall
> and our nightmares standing
> out there patiently waiting.[13]

I chanced upon A.T.B.'s post about blogger El Bashir Hazzam of Taghjijt, in Morocco's Guelmim province. El Bashir had blogged about a peaceful student demonstration and had also published the students' condemnation of the police's heavy-handed reaction, which reaction the police extended by placing Taghjijt under a curfew and closing local Internet cafés to prevent more news of the incident from reaching the outside world. El Bashir was charged with "spreading false information about human rights that undermined the kingdom's image" and sentenced to four months in prison.

I found El Bashir's Facebook page and quickly began communicating with his brother, Abdellah. El Bashir, now in jail, could only speak Arabic, but Abdellah, who was studying French at the university, was able to answer my questions.

In the process of the series of articles I wrote about El Bashir for the *Voice*, El Bashir went to court and was acquitted, due in part to the relatively large amount of public attention his case had garnered worldwide.

---

13 A. T. B., from poem "This American Dream" 2009

A shoe in the door

His thanks to me for doing my small part was gratifying, for sure, but I had a heap of music to explore. Abdellah continued communicating with me, sharing information about his region and the music played in his village, until his fiancée quite understandably demanded he stop texting with other women.

Back to the language site, where a sneaky request to practice French and learn Arabic won me several language partners from Morocco. I soon learned that nearly every region – sometimes every city – in Morocco had its own musical tradition, each as uniquely vibrant as its neighbor's, and that much of the music carried voices of resistance. This fact, combined with a tumultuous history, made the country look like a powder keg waiting to go off.

Most Moroccan youth were enamoured of the *raï* music of Algeria (more about that later), but one sent me an mp3 of some of the most haunting music I'd ever heard. A woman with a stirring voice sang a song in the role of the nurse of Prophet Mohamed. My source said the genre had been created by sub-Saharan slaves sold in Morocco. It was called "gnawa," a term I didn't remember having seen before, even in the afore-mentioned music guide. But it soon became clear that the "Sufi" music Louise Gray had described hearing in Marrakech had in fact been gnawa.

I was soon privileged to meet Driss Akjij, a fountainhead of Maghre-bian musical assistance. In the coming years it was Driss who helped me translate the Arabic and Amazigh dialects on the North African albums I was scribbling about, Driss who explained recent Moroccan music history, and Driss who suggested new artists.

Gnawa music developed when members of sub-Saharan tribes were forced to assimilate as slaves in Moroccan towns. The word "gnawa" refers to a black Muslim spiritual sect, and the name was derived from the me-dieval Maghreb belief that these slaves had originated in ancient Ghana.

The gnawa genre brings with it sub-Saharan musical modes, a hint of pre-Muslim Arab paganism, a Sufi predilection for inducing trance states, and a sense of alienation gleaned from centuries of being up-rooted and oppressed.

None of these elements can really be separated from gnawan music, although different groups will sometimes emphasize one element over the others. The Master Musicians of Joujouka, for example, tend to centre their performances around the chanting and trance rituals, while Izenzaren, like Nass El Gawain, focuses on the political message.

Gnawa holds much stylistic common ground with early American gospel and blues: call-and-response, a loose but salient rhythm structure, repetition, soulful delivery, coexisting spiritual and secular song subjects, expressions of intense emotions, crude and rustic instruments, and, often, musicians with no formal training.

There are also spiritual similarities. Like blues, gnawa has roots in pagan mysticism but sometimes upholds monotheism, paying homage to the Abrahamic God and to the teachings of Prophet Mohamed.

Musically gnawa is the African genre closest to the blues of North Mississippi, its modes rooted in the music of sub-Saharan slaves brought to America.

In addition to sharing some of the historical origins of blues, gnawa has had the same leavening influence as blues, galvanizing the development of other genres. Gnawa informs the thrilling hip hop songs of Morocco and Tunisia. It also uses blue notes (certain notes of the scale flattened slightly to create a soulful dissonance).

A premonition of upheaval

After tracing Morocco's musical dissent back to Nass El Gawain in the sixties and seeing how repressive the country could be today I became convinced that the unique history and cultural conditions of the Maghreb at this time were about to lead to some earth-shaking political changes.

I assumed this would begin in Morocco. I wasn't very surprised when the following year the first domino fell, but I was a little taken aback to see the unrest exploding first in Tunisia.

Love at the dawn of the Arab Spring

When people decide to live, destiny shall obey, and one day ... the slavery chains must be broken.
— Tunisian poet Abu Al-Qasem Al-Shabi

By November of 2010 I'd been separated from my first husband for eight months and had begun divorce proceedings. It was a month before the uprising began in Tunisia, and I was about to accidentally meet the Tunisian who was to change the course of my life.

On the invitation of Celia, an online friend from Brazil with whom I shared a love of all things Moroccan, I'd joined a European social network called Netlog. One night I opened the network to see a status update that was a quotation from Edgar Allan Poe, one of my favourite poets.

I immediately struck up a conversation with the man who'd posted it, who turned out to be a poet himself. We weren't able to talk long, and I didn't remember his name, but the next day when I opened the page again I saw a melancholy proverb which I was sure was his, with a picture that looked familiar. I texted a warm greeting.

"Who are you?" he texted back.

"I'm Wanda," I replied. "We spoke last night. You're the poet, right?"

"I'm not a poet. I'm a mechanic."

Disappointed, I tried to be polite, chatting a bit before signing off. I didn't like him at first, as he seemed cold and unfriendly. But in the following weeks if he saw me and had no one else to talk to he would greet me. I asked him about Tunisian music and he told me about *mezwed* (the Tunisian musical genre named after the country's peculiar bagpipe), sharing a few links. He grew on me, in part because he was so unromantic, so blunt, so sparing in warmth. Here was a guy I thought I could trust.

One day I texted him to ask about the political situation in Tunisia. "I know nothing of politics," he abruptly responded.

"I think you misunderstand me," I texted back.

"I understand you," he quickly replied. "I hope you can understand me."

I soon learned that the penalty for political dissidence in Tunisia was swift and severe, and that the Tunisian government under President Ben Ali was attempting to hack into all the Facebook accounts of the country's citizens.

December 17 came, and the self-immolation of vendor Mohamed Bouazizi became the catalyst for The Jasmine Revolution – the debut of the toppling effect soon to be named "The Arab Spring."

On January 3, 2011, the day students were to return to school after the holidays, a national strike was launched. More than eight Tunisian government websites were sabotaged by hackers as an expression of solidarity with the protesters.

I got in touch with blogger Lena Ben Mhenni, asking for anecdotes of Tunisian life under Ben Ali, and she shared the following:

> Some friends had invited me to a small party at their house. My host told me a story that his gardener had told him a few days ago. I asked to speak to the gardener, who explained that he was from a village in the Northwest of Tunisia. It had snowed there; the people needed aid from the government and the authorities had promised to provide the aid. On the day that the aid was provided, the TV was there to record and preserve this historic moment. But according to my witness, people were just handed some old wool blankets and some food, and as soon as the TV journalists left, the authorities took the items back.
>
> I can't say if this is typical, but it is not the first time that I have heard stories like this.

By January 10, 20 protesters had allegedly died in violent confrontations with police, and many police had been injured.

Nights in Tunisia

Two years later the country was slogging its way toward democracy and a kind of progress about which most Tunisians felt ambivalent. By then I'd married Ahmed Krimi and gone to live with him in Manouba, in northern Tunisia. No longer just dreaming of the Maghreb, I now lived there, soaking up the fresh and delicious Mediterranean cuisine, swimming in the bluest of seas, learning the customs of a culture that couldn't have been more different than my own.

On my first visit to Tunisia I'd attended my first traditional Tunisian wedding. I hadn't been prepared for the sight of women my grandmother's age sporting traditional desert garb, smiling joyfully while swinging their ample hips with shameless abandon to the sounds of the *mezwed*, *bindir*, and *dharbouka*. And here I'd thought all Arab Muslims were music-hating prudes.

My first mesmerizing musical experience in Tunisia arrived while we were still living in Nabeul. One morning I'd gotten up very early, just in time to hear all the mosques in the city making the call to prayer together. The polyphony was jarringly beautiful, a chance assembly of thrilling ancient sounds meeting, greeting, and dancing together through the lonely night.

Later when we lived in Manouba we visited a local café each night after supper, where we met Abdelkadr, better known as Gaddour. A friendly guy with a lot of friends, we didn't pay much notice to Gaddour until we saw him performing on television with his large *mezwed* ensemble, singing and playing a *bindir* (a lap drum like the Irish *bodhrán*, played with the hands) and *dharbouka* (an hourglass-shaped drum held between the thighs).

Mezwed is the indigenous musical genre of Tunisia, played on a kind of bagpipe made from the skin of a sheep or goat. (My husband refers to our bagpipe as "the Scottish mezwed"). The other defining feature is that mezwed music is based on traditional Amazigh rhythms, which Gaddour has clearly mastered.

Like blues, mezwed is a rural, working class mode of music that came to be embraced by all strata of society. It's now the music of choice popular at weddings and parties. There are special dances that accompany it, even a Sufi-inspired, trance-inducing, aggressive side-to-side stomp, piles of black hair whipped in violent circles.

Unlike some of the other African musicians I've interviewed, Gaddour hadn't been heavily influenced by American music. His listening had been pretty much restricted to mezwed and other Arab genres, as it had been for the musicians with whom he performed. This isn't quite as implausible as it sounds. Tunisia having been colonized by France until the sixties, French is the second language, and many music lovers simply restricted themselves to Arabic and French songs, not being able to understand the pop songs sung in English. Many of these musicians, including Gaddour, were unable to understand French, which restricted their listening to music from the Maghreb and perhaps a few other Arab regions.

Nonetheless, mezwed appears to have been open to outside influence. Today, due to the fact that the young are learning American English from movies on television, mezwed contains elements of rap and hip-hop, which isn't surprising; the songs resonate with the same obsessions, the issues uppermost in Tunisian hearts and minds: love, poverty, family relationships, immigration, and racism.

Gaddour informs me that no formal training exists for mezwed musicians; new musicians are taught within families or by friends. He came from a musical family, but being much younger than his siblings, no one had really had time to teach him, and so his education had come from friends, many of whom now perform with him in the grand ensemble, Golden Mezwed.

It's a little surprising to learn that the government does little to support this rich source of social and financial capital, even though in order to be permitted to perform publicly musicians must visit the Ministry of Culture and pass a musical exam every five years, after which they're awarded, if successful, a certificate of professionalism that opens doors to employment. The lack of government support may serve to keep the genre real, and thanks to a generous television industry that dotes on native music, many musicians are able to support themselves and their families without having to take second jobs.

Gaddour has been successful enough to land frequent local gigs, television appearances, and shows in Europe and North America, where he and Golden Mezwed perform for Tunisian expatriates yearning for the sounds of home.

Like much Middle Eastern music, in a typical performance the musicians play for a stretch, building excitement with increasingly faster rhythms and louder, more intense playing. When the singer arrives he or she and the audience are thoroughly prepped for an impassioned vocal performance.

Gaddour has played his *bindir* with Golden Mezwed at many traditional Tunisian festivities, including, he sheepishly admits, the celebration of the circumcision of the son of Ben Ali.

Each singer has a particular repertoire and subject matter; some focus on songs of love, some on loss, some on political struggles, some on poverty, and some on the joy of festivity. Like jazz musicians,

Gaddour and his musical colleagues must learn all of these repertoires by heart, both music and words, because they never know when they'll be called on to accompany this or that singer or even be asked to join in the singing. They're very much like jazz age studio musicians — walking fakebooks of all the popular standards of the day.

The technical aspects of mezwed the genre are easy to explain in words but in practice difficult to master. The rhythms are a combination of double beats and triplets that become more rapid and enmeshed as the music goes on. It's intoxicating to listen to a mezwed song start off slowly and then build in speed and intensity until you wonder if the musicians will be able to control it.

One thought that came back to me again and again while listening to these performances was how similar Tunisian music was to certain traditional forms of Celtic music. I still haven't found any scholarly work to establish a historical connection between North Africa and the Celtic peoples, but I can't help thinking that over the centuries the instrumentation, rhythms, harmonies, and musical motifs have somehow had occasion to meet and mingle.

At the edge of the world

> I have always loved the desert. One sits down on a desert sand dune, sees nothing, hears nothing. Yet through the silence something throbs, and gleams.
> —Antoine de Saint-Exupéry in *The Little Prince*

New Year's Day, 2016, found me standing at the edge of the Sahara, drinking in golden canyons radiant with the phantoms of the flora and fauna that had once thrived there, imagining the voices of peoples who'd traversed it for centuries.

The Sahara Desert long ago experienced several millennia of almost rainforest conditions. During this period humans began quitting the overpopulated Nile Valley to settle in the north of the African Peninsula. The mountain oasis of Mides in southwestern Tunisia is one of their settlements. It was given its name by ancient Roman colonizers who called it *Madés*.

We found several huts and booths advertising henna tattoos, green tea, and coffee. There were men there, young and old, who spent their days combing the area for the things we tourists covet but don't have the time to look for, things like fossils, petrified wood, and lovely bloomlike gypsum formations called "desert roses," all of which were displayed for sale on wooden tables.

The village sat on the large gorge used for the desert scenes in *The English Patient*. This gorge served as a defence in earlier years, and looked like rather a dangerous place for children to play, like the abandoned Pueblo communities of the American Southwest that had a similar history of lush beginnings fading to arid inhabitability. People continued to live in Mides until 1969, when 22 days of rain washed away most of their houses.

More than anything I wanted to know what kind of music had been heard here.

We were accompanied by a young man, allegedly our guide but who remained silent until we reached the summit of the hill, where he cut me off from the herd. I was the only Westerner in the group and so it was assumed I had money I wanted to spend. He directed me to a display of necklaces, drawing my attention to an intriguing pendant, explaining that he'd bought it from Tuaregs with whom he traded at the Algerian border.

The Tuareg symbol has many forms, each peculiar to the town in which the wearer was born, but they all consist of a round circle topping a kind of cross. There are many theories and explanations of the historical meaning of this symbol, sometimes called the "Tuareg Southern Cross" or the "Cross of Agadez" (named after the city in Niger). For me the hollow circle and the cross have taken on a special significance. But I'll explain all that later.

I'd been infatuated with all things Tuareg ever since having been first introduced to Tinariwen by Driss Akjij, I bought it on the spot, for the equivalent of 12 Canadian dollars. Ahmed later told me I'd paid too much, but my rule was always to pay the same or less than what I'd pay for a similar item in Canada and not to worry my head over the paleface premium.

> The desert could not be claimed or owned – it was a piece of cloth carried by winds, never held down by stones, and given a hundred shifting names ... Its caravans, those strange rambling feasts and cultures, left nothing behind, not an ember. All of us, even those with European homes and children in the distance, wished to remove the clothing of our countries. It was a place of faith. We disappeared into landscape.
> —Michael Ondaatje, *The English Patient*

I was still intensely curious as to why the Sahara should be the historical origin of so much phenomenal world music including blues, rock, jazz, Celtic tunes, European fado, rembetika, and flamenco, chaabi, North African raï, gnawa, and mezwed, forming a helix in which music goes out and comes back, like spawning salmon, returning to its roots to inspire and be inspired again and again.

One element of the desert's creative power is its longstanding occupation by Berber tribes, an ethnic group indigenous to the region from long before the arrival of Arabs.[14] This is where we get the root of the word "barbarian," as the Romans remarked that the speech of these

---

14 https://www.britannica.com/topic/Berber

peoples was heavy with the sound "bar-bar." The more accurate name for this Afro-Asiatic ethnic group is "Amazigh." Amazigh cultures still thrive in the Sahara and North Africa despite having mixed with Arabs to the point where their DNA is nearly identical, but culturally they're as different as Celts from Saxons.

The term Amazigh also applies to many subgroups, including the Tuaregs, the Kabyles, and a subgroup of Jews (called Djerba Berbers because of the island in Tunisia where they've lived for more than 2500 years). The Amazigh are famous arts lovers, adoring dance, music, fine textiles, elegant architecture, personal adornment, and good food. At the same time their history shows them to be fierce and uncompromising, and their longstanding practice of slave-trading, even selling members of their own tribes, was the brutal means by which North African rhythms, instrumentation, modes, and tonalities entered North America.

The Amazigh weren't the only group to exert great influence on world music (the Sub-Saharan Hausa peoples had a huge part in the development of gnawa) and yet their influence eclipses that of most others because of the control they exerted over the Saharan trade routes. Because of their love of music and their command of the desert's crossroads, the Amazigh helped spread the different musical genres born and refined at the desert's heart.

The desert has never been a welcoming place. The countries in and around the Sahara all have histories of violent struggle with European colonizers. In addition, criminal and extremist groups have for a long time and today continue to hide themselves and carry out nefarious deeds there.

The difficulty (if not hopelessness) of policing the unsettled regions has always made unguarded exploration a treacherous undertaking, and then there's the danger of dying for want of food, water, and shade. Some true accounts, for example Captain James Riley's 19th century *Sufferings in Africa*, paint a harrowing picture of long forced treks through the desert at the mercy of heartless kidnappers.

But many voyages through the Sahara were made under more favourable conditions. Ever since the Prophet Mohamed began instructing his followers to make pilgrimages to Mecca, millions of Sub-Saharan and North African Muslims have journeyed through this desert en route to the Holy City. I've talked to several Muslims who weren't particularly religious before taking this pilgrimage but who afterwards claimed the trip was a life-changer. Imagine following such an experience with weeks of trekking through the silence of desert! Having been to Mecca, what must it have been like to digest the experience during a lengthy camel ride through such a hauntingly beautiful landscape, with no diversion but a few hand drums, flutes, stringed instruments, and storytellers around the evening fire?

Though owing much to its history it was clear that the Sahara's power to move and to inspire music and poetry was largely grounded in the geography itself. I for one wanted to stay there forever, to see what poetry and music I might be inspired to create.

Blues soundquest

Years ago I'd undertaken a soundquest in search of the essence of blues. After hearing elements of it in other music I learned what it was and started looking for purer, more distilled versions. I'd been hearing sounds that had simply hinted at what I wanted to hear, like bread crumbs in the woods leading Hansel and Gretel back home. I kept thinking, *Yeah, like that, but more – more of those bent notes and dissonant chords, more of those sad lyrics, more of that moaning voice.*

It was 1981 in the record library of CKDU, Dalhousie University's radio station, that I came to the blues zenith of my soundquest, which came in the form of a field recording of sharecropper R.L. Burnside singing and playing his guitar. Burnside lived in northern Mississippi, often called the "Mississippi hill country," a region harboring a large number of musicians who played a distinctive form of blues.

At that time Burnside hadn't ever been in a sound studio and so was far from the electronic experimentation that characterized his later work. In this field recording it was just Burnside at home with his guitar and lots of kids clacking away on whatever household objects could be used as rhythm instruments.

Later I learned that the reason this music sounded so strange to the Western ear and what made it so different from all other incarnations of the blues was that it lacked the 12 or 16-bar structure. Twelve-bar blues was an African-American innovation, a kind of compromise between West African music and the AABA structure at the heart of the European song tradition.

Burnside was different, and it wasn't just him. There was a long-standing musical subgenre in the Mississippi hill country, a region whose blues forms heavily influenced but didn't supplant what we now call Mississippi Delta Blues. The blues musicians of northern Mississippi played *modal* music.

What is modal music? Here's the dummy's guide: modal music is comprised of one basic riff played over and over again in slightly different forms until a completely different and mesmerizing riff, which is only repeated a few times, comes along.

How many times do you repeat the musical motif? I assume that some master's student has actually addressed this question, but not being a scholar, I can only guess. When I listen to modal music I can hear roughly where it should change, and the change always feels right. But if I count the number of times the first motif is played, it's never the same number – the riff doesn't change after a set number of repetitions, but it does change in response to rises in musical tension.

As for the lyrics of modal blues songs, they're thematically similar to those of mainstream blues – the supplicant moans, the groanings that cannot be uttered, the lion's roar of love and despair, the *double entendre*, the stream-of-consciousness narratives.

The bent notes on the third and the sixth tone of the scale and the dissonant chords sound characteristically bluesy, but the sound is a far cry from B.B. King, Muddy Waters, or Etta James, or even from Bessie Smith, whose career predated Burnside's by decades but whose blues style was a more recent development than Burnside's more primal sound.

When fans of this music listen to the indigenous music of West Africa they're blown away by the similarity – that same loose modal form, the twirling, winding, mellifluous riffs, the complex rhythms, the sweetly dissonant chords, and the soft vocals. It's so distinct from the style common in urban blues clubs that you almost forget that they're also referred to as blues.

The regions within and around Mali have long been believed to be the homes of those African cultures most likely to have passed on their musical codes. They sent them with the slaves shipped to North Africa, and the closest form of American music to Mali's is the blues of the Mississippi hill country.

> The blues is at the root of all the music I grew up loving ... At the root of the blues is Africa, and at the root of the African root of the blues is Mali.
> —Markus James

Things have gone full circle. The musicians in the Tuareg group Tinariwen listened to Santana, Jimi Hendrix, Led Zeppelin, Bob Marley, Dire Straits, and others, but these American artists had all been distantly influenced by the music of the slaves that had arrived on their shores from west Africa.

There's more commonality between the musical aspects of both Saharan and hill country blues. One example is the combination of instruments – flute, stringed instrument, and drum – heard in Mississippi fife and drum bands of the turn of the 19th and 20th centuries.

The *assouf* guitar style, like blues guitar, also proceeded naturally from the acoustic to the electric guitar, which emphasized certain elements in the music, like sustain, that had tended to lie dormant under acoustic strings but which became clearer with amplification. Particularly noteworthy was the intensity engendered by the hammer runs and dissonant chords.

There's a vocal call and response running through the blues traditions (made more manifest in gospel music) which is a part of the desert tradition as well.

Another feature of both American blues and desert blues is their profound cultural influence within their own regions. It's impossible to imagine 20th-century American pop music without the cornerstone of blues, which spawned or influenced the development of jazz, ragtime, gospel, barrelhouse, honky-tonk, bluegrass, Cajun, cabaret, rock and roll, rhythm and blues, soul, hip hop, and other genres.

Similarly, it's hard to imagine North African popular music of the 20th century without the fertilizing influence of Saharan music. There's an ongoing circle of influence in the North African countries that connects the music of the Saharan Tuareg and Wodaabe tribes to the development of gnawa, raï, chaabi, Andalusian music, African reggae, Ahwach, and many others.

Many of these North African musical genres have had international influences, but so had early blues, whose tones were altered in response to the sound of bagpipes, Hawaiian guitar, and the simple beats, modal chants, and ululations of Native American music. And we must also acknowledge the influence of the various noisemakers constructed by children from discarded objects like soda cans and bottles, cigar boxes, pipes, jugs, and discarded wire.

As a child, Tinariwen's founder, Ibrahim Ag Elabib, threw together homemade instruments,[15] as had children in the Deep South (and the rural Nova Scotia of my childhood). And he's said to have witnessed his father's execution, just as many children in the American South had witnessed the lynchings of their fathers. Like the blues musicians, the Tuareg and Wodaabe tribes were forced to endure repressive racist governments and condemning social mores.

Saharan musicians tended to form loose collectives instead of bands, much like the northern Mississippi blues musicians, who tended to centre musical alliances around homes and juke joints. The religious similarities included an intense spirituality more animist than monotheistic.

The blues aesthetic embraces strangeness, the occult, tragedy, alienation, despair, rejection, violence, and raw sexual desire. The Saharan musical aesthetic is remarkably similar, holding an image of the musician as a marginalized forerunner of social change.

The crossroads

There's also the Jungian metaphorical similarity. Blues musicians have a legend about meeting a dark man at a crossroads, a man who in exchange for your soul will teach you how to become a guitar wizard. Here

---

15   https://www.guitarplayer.com/miscellaneous/ibrahim-ag-alhabib-of-tinariwen

the crossroads metaphor signifies the juncture at which the musician crosses over from the banal world of study and repetitious practice and into the world of music's magical power. You hand the mysterious man your guitar, he tunes it, shows you a couple of licks, steals your soul, and all's well that ends well until you realize that you've traded eternity for the doubtful privilege of being a guitar god.

The crossroads is the landing point of a tornado, the meeting place of currents of passion that collide and spiral upwards. The Tuareg pendant I still wear speaks of it, holding in its image the circle of life, the cross of Golgotha, and the universal juncture of two realities.

There's something profoundly meaningful in this notion of a crossroads, a meeting place between two or more worlds, carnal and spiritual, pale and dark, northern and southern, government and grassroots, freedom and authority, black and white, Arab and Amazigh. It's of significance to Saharan musical traditions, which have developed in response to that peculiar mix of cultures throwing sparks at the juncture between the Arab North and sub-Saharan South. It's just as meaningful to the American experience, where the crossroads symbolizes, among other things, the place where the imperialist European confronts his accuser — the kidnapped and enslaved African whose soul he's wronged.

> Standin' at the crossroad, babe,
> risin' sun goin' down ...
> I believe to my soul now,
> Poor Bob is sinkin' down ...
> — Robert Johnson, "Crossroad Blues"

The long shadow of myth

Karl Marx was wrong; life did not *completely* change in response to the screeching gears of the age of industry. As recent wars and revolutions have shown, we're still living in the shadows of Abraham, Isaac, and Ishmael, of Achilles and Hector, of Nefertiti and Tutankhamun, of Burnt Njall.

As Northrop Frye wrote nearly 30 years ago in *The Great Code*, the poet's role is to keep primitive language modes alive in the flux, ephemera, and scientific reasoning typical of the Industrial Age. There are poetic spaces on this planet that bear up well under this responsibility.

Let's compare these blues lyrics from Lonnie Johnson ...

> So tired of sighin'
> So tired of cryin'
> I'm so tired of livin' all alone.
> All my days seem weary.
> The skies seem dreary.
> And I'm all alone and where must I roam?

... with those of an old nomad poem from the anthology *al-Majani al-haditha*, published in 1946:

> I am tired of the burdens of life; make no mistake, whoever lives to
> fourscore years grows tired.
> I know what is happening today and what happened yesterday, but
> I cannot tell what tomorrow will bring.
> I have seen the Fates stamp like a camel in the dark; those they touch
> they kill, and those they miss live on to grow old.

Islam reached the pagan nomadic tribes because of Sufis who travelled the Sahara spreading their own mystical version of the religion. The desert tribes, because of constant travelling and a desperate daily struggle for survival, often found it impossible to keep to the rigorous schedule of prayers, charitable donations, mosque visits, and pilgrimages more suited to the settled villager. Their lives were more adaptable to Sufism, with its emphasis on mystical experience and attentiveness to God and its acceptance of music as a viable part of religious worship.

Today there are more than three and a half million Tuareg divided across five North African countries. Though Muslim, their society is matrilineal, and the men are veiled while the women are not. They travel by camel, these days by truck and jeep as well, and are still highly dependent on herds for their sustenance. As is common for such highly specialized cultures, the progress of industry has upset the balance of their lives, and conflicts within and among the nation states in which they live have threatened their safety.

The Tuareg tend to be tall, slim, and beautiful, with haunting facial features. There appears a greater-than-average physical difference between the men (tall and lanky) and the women (round and voluptuous) but this may be due to their markedly different daily activities. Skin colour varies; there are a few nearly as pale as Northern Europeans and others who look like sub-Saharan Africans. They make gorgeous jewellery, music, and clothing, and have a rich storytelling heritage, with *griots* playing a major role in passing on communal wisdom.

For more than 2000 years it was the Tuareg — the herdsman, artisans, musicians, warriors, and travelling salesmen of the desert — who controlled trade in the Sahara.

The Tuareg have sought refuge from persecution for decades, forced to accept the agenda of the countries in which they reside as refugees, with, sometimes, disastrous long-term results. The French colonizers exploited them, and then, when Mali gained independence from France 50 years ago, the process of annihilation simply changed hands. Libya's Muammar Gaddafi employed Tuareg refugees to help him hold on to power, and when the dictator fell Libya's national army came after the Tuaregs in revenge, obliging many to return to Mali, where the menacing face of Islamic extremism kept their tranquility at bay.

The Tuareg being a nomadic society, with no solid network or infrastructure, governments tend to feel free to ignore agreements, promises, and obligations. In the case of Mali, the neglect has long comprised what looks like slow genocide.

So far the genocide has failed, as has the silencing of the Tuareg voice. The hypnotic rhythms and soulful vocals of Tuareg music – not to mention its representation of the outcast – puts it among the more primary influences on Algeria's raï music, the Maghreb's youthful cry of rebellion against stifling laws and social mores.

Aïcha, Aïcha

Ooh! Aïcha, Aïcha, écoute-moi. Aïcha, Aïcha, t'en vas pas. Aïcha, Aïcha, regarde-moi.
Aïcha, Aïcha, réponds-moi.

In 1996 the iconic raï singer Cheb Khaled released "Aïcha," which he sang in French and Arabic. It topped the charts in the Maghreb and much of Europe, where it remained a hit until at least 2003.

In this song a man vows to smother his love object in jewels and other niceties if only she'll stay with him forever. She refuses him. And what a refusal:

"Keep your treasures.
I'm worth more than all the
Bars are bars, even if
    made of gold."

Ooh! Aïcha, Aïcha, écoute-moi. Aïcha, Aïcha, t'en vas pas. Aïcha, Aïcha,
regarde-moi.

To my disappointment, when I came to live in the Arab world I found young girls whose sole hope lay in nailing a rich husband. Having in their possessions even a small token of the Western "utopia" was a sign of status, even when it insulted who they were, belittling their beauty and dismissing their pain.

Ooh! Aïcha, Aïcha, écoute-moi. Aïcha, Aïcha, t'en vas pas. Aïcha, Aïcha, regarde-moi.
Aïcha, Aïcha, réponds-moi.

Later, in Montreal, I met an Algerian ex-pat who explained that raï music is socially redemptive, airing, in the harmless context of music, the longings, resentments, frustrations, and despair that the Arab dares not speak.

Much like the euphemisms we find in early black American folk tales and songs at once disguising reality and revealing it.

In this view the words of "Aïcha" ring powerfully true, flying in the face of the prevailing social moralities:

I want the same rights as you
And respect for each day.
I don't want anything but love."

Ooh! Aïcha, Aïcha, écoute-moi. Aïcha, Aïcha, t'en vas... Aïcha, Aïcha, regarde-moi.
...pas Aïcha, Aïcha, réponds-moi.

Why raï?

By the time I heard Rachid Taha perform at the Olympia Theatre in Montreal in 2013 I'd come to see musical syncretism – the mixing of various genres – as an operating principle in music, something that music's natural evolution required. As pertains to this age, if any genre could be seen as dominant, and if it could be called a genre, syncretism was it. It was that part of music that reached out for wholeness and oneness. It was peace emerging as an insistent voice from within music itself.

With raï the Arab exile reached out and embraced not only their brothers and sisters, but all of Europe. The musical descendent of all North African genres, raï brought the Sahara to the North and the West, claiming and internalizing the disparate musical genres it found on its way.

The punk rock of Arab exile

In the early '80s Rachid Taha did lead vocals for the French rock group *Carte de Sejour*. Identifying with the sense of estrangement expressed by the burgeoning punk rock movement and taking advantage of the anything-goes freedom of '80s music, he sang in French, English, and Arabic. In 1986 he chose a standard patriotic French song, *"Douce France,"* singing the words with a searing sarcasm that clearly condemned Western political conservatives. His song targeted those who extolled the virtues of family life while promoting policies that contributed to the destruction of families in foreign countries – and to measures that ghettoized the foreigners within their own borders.

It hit a little too close to home, and the song was banned from French radio.

Taha has often presented the West with annoying in-your-face reminders of the colonialism that created a generation adrift, destitute at home and abroad, belonging nowhere. The anthem of the exiled Arab, echoing the bitterness inherent in blues, reggae, and folk music, already has universal undertones. In the wake of the Arab Spring, it's becoming more and more the common experience of humanity, and perhaps for this reason the songs of Taha have been so enthusiastically embraced the world over.

The Algerian in Paris is brother to the homeless Ojibwa wandering the streets of Toronto, the Syrian family fleeing for their lives, and the thousands more driven from their homelands and refused entry to one nation after another.

The way of all music

It's slightly odd that raï seems to have been left to its own genre-marrying devices with no resistance from its followers. From the dawn of history musical traditions have been developing via contact with neighboring tribes, pushing aside natural prejudices to embrace sounds new and strange, yet such a natural and inevitable process rarely escapes the hue and cry of musical purists who think of *their* genre as spotless and all-of-a-piece, believing it to have arrived at the dawn of time in the same shape they find it in today. We got this kind of resistance from haters of fusion jazz, from the folk Nazis who despised Bob Dylan the moment he pulled out an electric guitar, and from the people who sneered at Van Morrison for singing Celtic songs with a bluesy inflection.

So where were the raï purists? Where was the anger when raï artists travelled the world, mixing raï with blues, rock, reggae, and heaven knows what else? Why, when raï artists began leaving Oran for Europe and elsewhere, did no one say, "Wait a minute, they're mixing raï with hip hop – that's not done!"

Here's an even bigger question: What drove the raï artists to pursue every opportunity to meld their music with the most engaging world genres they could find? Sure, syncretism happens, but usually it happens slowly, as if by chance, against a tide of resistance. The raï musicians displayed an unusual taste for collaboration and genre-blending as well as a haste to get it done, as if there might not be any more music next week.

Raï's roots go deep, but it first began developing its distinctive form in the late 1920's, around the time Jelly Roll Morton was recording his albums and Tin Pan Alley was still churning out lighthearted American hits. Raï emerged among the poor in cities like Oran, near the Mediterranean Sea, a region that has long dished up a mulligan stew of European, African, and American musical influences – just like New Orleans. But raï didn't enter worldwide notice until the musical experiments of the 1980s allowed the careers of the best-known raï artists to take off and go mainstream.

In its moving and morphing raï wasn't alone. The same thing was happening with India's bhangra tradition, which saw most of its development taking place at Indian weddings in the British Isles. It was also happening with many genres of Hispanic and Portuguese music.

I just heard an interesting little documentary on the CBC about how we came to have the "Chinese" food we enjoy in Canada today. As it turns out, egg rolls and chow mein as we know them aren't traditional Chinese foods at all but rather were invented by Chinese immigrants who hadn't learned to cook back in China and were unable to find the right ingredients in their adopted country. They created dishes with a Chinese flavour, using Canadian ingredients and adapted to the Canadian palate.

It struck me that a similar process had been undertaken with music. Rachid Taha, Cheb Khaled, and their cohorts had left North Africa young, and some had even been born abroad, having never mastered the musical traditions of their fatherlands. What they brought to Europe was the essential flavour of the Maghreb, interpreted through their own personal experiences of exile in Europe.

Beauty from ashes

Although leaving seemed like the only choice, many Middle Eastern immigrants saw they'd jumped from the frying pan into the fire when, after fleeing to European countries, they found that Islamist extremists had beaten them there and that between the extremists and the European racists their lives had only nominally improved.

This kind of dilemma will make anybody sing the blues. And from within these blues emerges a voice so deep, so compassionate, so ancient and beautiful that it's a pearl of great price, something to offer your soul for. The fact that one has a wretched life in the new land but nothing to go back to puts double spurs to artistic creativity. You have two choices: lie down and die or get to work making something amazing to lift you out of your misery.

It was their distinctive cultural backgrounds as well as the experience of exile that drove Rachid Taha, Cheb Khaled, and many other Arab musicians to take poverty and racial oppression and turn them into artistic opportunity.

Taha saw exile as the event that had delivered to him the manifold treasures of world culture:

Since I started making music I've worked with some very interesting people, some in the field of techno-progressive music listening, and at the same time I've been listening to Arab singers like Oum Kalthoum. I've also listened to a lot of intellectuals, writers, and painters, who've enriched me by helping me evolve. This is my wealth.
— Rachid Taha, interview 2013

But in "Algerian Tango," Taha sings of his deep wound:

I can't forget the past,
the racists, or those who enslave us.
I've opened my eyes and my heart,
and have given you everything,
and you have lied to me.

"What's the answer to this kind of pain?" I asked him.
His reply was immediate:
"The solution is love."

Finding the desert's voice at last

Earlier I wrote that when I visited Mides I'd longed to hear the music played there when it had been inhabited.

With me and Ahmed in Mides were his sister, Hounaida, and her husband Mohamed. The couple had married back in September, at a traditional seven-day Tunisian wedding. On the third day Hounaida's grandmother and aunts had dressed her in traditional garb and instructed her to rest quietly. She sat on a little canopied couch, surrounded by friends and family on floor mattresses.

Soon the older women began to sing loud, wailing harmonies in a minor key. I asked the others what the women were singing about, but no one knew – this dialect was too old, and only the old women understood it.

It didn't matter; it was the essence of all the Arab music I'd heard up until then, a wind howling through the dunes, a hawk's cry, a camel's groaning complaint. It was love of family wrapped in a primal restlessness, a lament of loss and abandonment.

Looking out over the Sahara I recalled this wedding and realized I'd already heard the desert's voice among these women. The pinnacle of this phase of my soundquest had been reached, and I could now go home.

Driving away from Mides we wouldn't have known the wind was rising had we not seen pockets of date palms waving violently *en masse*. Such motion seemed all the more striking within a setting of broad vistas of motionless rock and sand. It was like staring at a roomful of statues and seeing a few of them begin to dance to the sound of an invisible mezwed.

Soundtrack for an age of pain

My Jazz Years

In 2007 I got a tenor banjo.

I'd wanted a five-string.

At the Digby music store I asked Tommy Cowan what kind of music was played on a tenor banjo.

Dixieland!

I told Josh Peck, who loved Dixieland as much as I did.

Let's start a band!!

We were lame at first, but we got better, and other people started joining us.

We practiced religiously at the front of the church every Tuesday night. Called ourselves "The Dixie Hicks."

It was blissful.

One new musician was clarinetist Jack Malmstrom.

Jack later backed me at spoken word events.

Angst! Ennui! Void! Despair!

He recruited me to his project, which also included his wife Susan on drums—

"The Radio Stardust Jazz Orchestra."

I learned to comp. We played in bars and art galleries, and started recording an album.

Jazz was the only bright spot in those dark years.

I'd also enjoyed playing sacred music, folk, bluegrass, and blues.

But they couldn't hold a candle to the joy of playing jazz with other musicians. Why not?

What was it about jazz?

by Wanda Waterman

105

Montreal jazz guitarist and university professor Michael Gauthier shared this anecdote, so illustrative of the mysterious quality in music that makes it intrinsic to human experience:

> Back in the eighties there was an el primo jazz club in Montreal called The Rising Sun. Sonny Stitt, the famous bebop alto sax player, was playing there with a local band that included my friend, Art Roberts, on the piano. Art invited me to come see the show for free, so of course I went, and during the break Art invited me upstairs to hang out with the other musicians. He introduced me to Sonny, but after that I just sat there like a peanut, saying nothing, just listening to all these guys in their forties and fifties talking together.
>
> Suddenly Sonny turned to me and said, 'Mike [he'd remembered my name!], they can take your woman, they can take your house, they can take your money, but they can never take your music. Never forget that.'
>
> It was like God had spoken to me. It affirmed what I already suspected to be true.
>
> —Michael Gauthier, interview 2014

The dawnings of cool

Sonny Stitt didn't need to impress anyone. He appeared dispassionate, but his output revealed an almost superhuman focus. He'd bravely forged ahead with his original style as if he'd had nothing to lose. He was aware of injustice but knew it was here to stay and that he had better things to focus on than protest. He dressed well and had poise. And as the above anecdote illustrates, he had his priorities right. He recognized that man's life's a vapor, filled with woes, and that the wisest response was to keep his dignity and poise intact and live life on his own terms.

That's kind of what cool is.

I've already talked about the terrorism of our time, which most white folks today think of as a new phenomenon, a vague threat that renders them chronically uneasy, unnerved by the heightened danger of attack by foreign hostiles.

How quickly we forget that African North Americans have been terrorist victims from the beginnings of their forced sojourns here.

If for even a moment we could get our heads around living under the shadow of white-hooded mobs and burning crosses in the night, deadly beatings, the witnessing of the murders of family members, lying accusations ending in life sentences or death, disenfranchisement, rape, segregation, poverty, and humiliation, we might snicker at the spectacle of a conservative white politician waving his fists in opposition to the admission of Syrian refugees.

We might also begin to understand how terribly hard-won jazz really was and how the horrendous difficulty of its beginnings played a role in its enduring, encompassing beauty.

Without jazz we wouldn't have cool. Without cool, jazz would be incomprehensible. Cool doesn't make a distinction between high and low art; all things are one in cool. Cool embraces a sense of freedom, newness, openness, a rejection of hierarchical power structures, a personal elegance, and a special membership within an exclusive elite. Cool is both an aesthetic and a personal attitude.

Cool emerged from the phase of American jazz culture that came after World War II. Cool was quickly embraced the world over by youth who saw cool as the way they were or ought to be. And ever since then nearly every serious movie hero has personified cool.

Cool was an inconspicuously rebellious stance that on the surface looked like an unflappable calm, a demeanour that steadfastly resisted humiliation or control by outside forces. It was an impossible ideal, mostly only in reach of the ethnic group that had suffered so much that almost nothing could hurt, fool, or scare it anymore. But when the youth in the rest of the world saw it they knew it was for them.

Not all jazz musicians were cool. If I had to make up my own personal list I'd say Miles Davis, Ornette Coleman, John Coltrane, Lester Young, Chet Baker, and Billie Holiday were cool. Brilliant artists though they were, Benny Goodman, Louis Armstrong, and Ella Fitzgerald were not cool – they were just too perky and ingratiating. Bebop jazz and the free jazz it lead to were cool; Dixieland, swing, and crooners were not cool. Being a musician was cool, but selling out to the industry was not. Cab Calloway, though marketed as cool wasn't truly cool because he also was too perky, and besides, he stood in the way of musical innovation. Dizzy Gillespie and Charlie Parker were cooler. Communism was not cool, but talking about it while wearing a black turtleneck, drinking espresso, and chain-smoking in a café definitely was. Realist art was cool only when it was unsentimental and carried a dissident message. *Avant-garde* art was cool almost by definition.

Yes, cool was hard-won, which may explain its staying power. Cool was born not only of unconscionable violence against an ethnic group but of all the daily slights, the reminders of the inferior status they held, the constant bruising of human pride, the condescension from less intelligent beings. These circumstances lead to an explosion of self-actualization, of dignity, of a blasé "to hell with them" mentality. The world slowly recognized the value of this fearless stance and encouraged its development as it spread. Cool was essential to making America the pop culture hub of the world.

Cool remained even after jazz left the musical mainstream, forever intertwined with popular culture in the West. It became the standard by which we judged ourselves, one of the criteria being a steadfast remaining true to self, even if that meant leaving jazz behind.

No more zeitgeist

When I asked pianist Neil Cowley why his compositions had slowly moved away from jazz and toward more personal innovation, he replied:

> My love of jazz came from things that swing. I listened to Erroll Garner as a kid. I adore playing that stuff and I'm actually good at it, but I no longer do it openly, because I don't think it fits with how we're living now. It feels like it comes from an age gone by, and I wish it wasn't. It would be glorious for music to be that happy, but it's just not the zeitgeist of the age now.
> —Neil Cowley, interview 2017

Were times really happier, or is that simply what the music lead us to believe? Listening to early Jelly Roll Morton and Louis Armstrong somehow makes us forget Jim Crow and the two World Wars. The music owes some of its sublime cheeriness to the white middle and upper classes who demanded black musical artists reflect back to them their own gauzily romantic vision of their safe, privileged existences.

The early recordings of Duke Ellington, Charlie Parker, and Bennie Goodman temporarily erased awareness of the Great Depression and World War II, at least while you were listening. You just don't hear war and famine in those tunes. If jazz was happy, it may not have been because jazz makers had something to smile about but rather because our mental health depended on the distraction of such playful creativity to keep it from sinking.

What Cowley was suggesting, at least from the gist of the rest of our conversation, was that he and other artists are no longer quite so ready to pretend everything is fine. That's getting old.

I can dig it. As much as I believe in the value of the music that cheered up the world during two wars, a depression, and decades of social tragedy, of profound letdowns from the powers that be – hiding all that behind a veneer of happy-go-lucky songs isn't doable anymore. Jazz spawned cool at the height of its achievement, but cool changed the direction of jazz. No more gilding the lily; it just wasn't cool.

In Cowley's case cool has most definitely outlived jazz to form an integral part of the zeitgeist. His original compositions are vibrant with ear-engaging chords and progressions, melodies and rhythms, but in his 2016 album *Spacebound Apes* you can hear a marked departure from the jazz of his 2006 debut album.

For the purposes of jazz festivals his music is still called jazz even though it no longer swings and now follows different chord progressions. He creates beautiful instrumental pieces that speak of a deep malaise, a sense of discouragement, and a poignant longing for freedom. His explanations behind the story of *Spacebound Apes* can be found in a comic book tale of a simian astronaut named Lincoln. How cool is that? If I had to draw a parallel, I'd have to say that Cowley's music is more exemplary of the rural blues period in jazz history as opposed to the big band era. But in consideration of the aforementioned vortex, such parallels are really a thing of the past.

Where's our scene?

So what's the *zeitgeist* music of our age? How has music responded to the emotional, psychological, and spiritual needs of listeners in the last two decades?

Cowley and I tried to figure it out, naming Robert Glasper, Marco Benevento, and various other interesting new experiments before agreeing that none of these could be called a "scene" in the sense of a musical genre presiding over the entertainment industry the way Tin Pan Alley, big band, bebop, free jazz, rock music, and punk had done in their times. From the beginning of the new millennium geniuses had appeared, and more were still emerging, but these were all working along on their own, as Cowley did in his little garden studio, braving lonely hours to do justice to the musical messages burgeoning inside him, messages he could no longer couch in the language of jazz or pigeonhole according to any nameable *scene*.

It hadn't happened overnight. I remember in the late eighties a magazine spread about the video jockey team on MuchMusic, each one listing their favourite bands. None of the bands were the same and none were any I'd ever heard of. People were no longer proud to say the Beatles were their favourite band — that was passé. What was cool was finding music just for you, from artists you could relate to personally.

It was clear that by the year 2000 the postmodern world, though rife with originality, was done with "scenes."

Changing voices

Cowley told me about a man he knew whose soundquest had obliged him to take great pains assembling the best phonograph system money could buy, even ordering parts from overseas. When at last he'd felt it was ready he'd put on a Joni Mitchell LP and closed his eyes.

He had arrived. He could swear that Joni was standing right there, singing to him alone. It was enough. After that he scrapped the whole sound system, cherishing this precious memory of the zenith of his listening experience.

As for why the man would chuck such an amazing system without at least listening to Jesse Mae Hemphill on it, well, we'll just have to chalk that up to the eccentricity of the leisured class. The man had been true to his soundquest, and that's what mattered.

Piles of folks can boast of having heard Joni Mitchell sing, having obtained the privilege years ago for the price of a concert ticket, or even without having paid a dime if they were lucky enough to have jammed with Joni or been her pal. But I imagine there was something quite special about getting this experience from a piece of vinyl.

I can dig it; I miss the whole vinyl experience, with its full, sonorous scratchiness and the delight of sitting on your friends' bedroom floors as they treated you to a retrospective of their older siblings' record collections. I miss the whole idea of LP records as art forms with story arcs, great cover art, and room for stickers, buttons, posters, and reefer paper.

Today, Cowley pointed out, there were groups that met to listen reverently to vinyl albums, discussing them just as reverently afterwards, as if the age of vinyl had been a time of prophets, a sacred epoch on which to found centuries of worship.

Not for this crowd

In 2012, shortly after Gil Scott-Heron had passed away, jazz baritone Giacomo Gates put out a CD of Heron's songs, calling it *The Revolution Will Be Jazz*. The album was a genuine and beautifully executed tribute to one of the most underpaid and undersung heroes of American music. Despite their being the sparks that had eventually ignited rap music, Heron's songs and poems got little airplay because they were just a little too challenging to the worldview fabricated to maintain the status quo (just listen to "Whitey on the Moon").

I met Gates at the bar of an upscale summer resort in Laconia, on New Hampshire's Lake Winnipesaukee. The performance was remarkable, if a little predictable: a set of standards, a few reminiscences, and Gates's rich, deep voice accompanied by the brilliant Berklee alumni Bruce Gertz, John Funkhouser, and Jonathan Lorentz.

During the intermission Gates apologetically confessed that he couldn't do any of the Gil-Scott Heron songs for this crowd. And of course he couldn't. Genres like jazz, old timey music, raï , tango, fado, and blues may have originated among slaves, the poor, the exiles, and the disenfranchised, but once a genre becomes gentrified its voice changes along with its audience.

If jazz were ever to truly die, it would be here, among these wealthy New England vacationers who love the sophisticated chords, the delightful rhythms, and the masterful musicians, but reject the social message, clinging to the power structures cool rejects.

This was no worry for those of us who knew we had all of jazz available to us. Besides, between the Neil Cowleys who laid jazz aside but stayed cool and the New Hampshire sophisticates who preferred their jazz uncool there was still real jazz being made. And thanks to the new technologies the full spectrum of jazz was as close as our earbuds. Those who chose to seek it out could find all the jazz they wanted. And those who wanted to and who worked hard enough could play it any which way they pleased. Or, like Cowley, they could just stay cool and move on.

I asked Michael Gauthier if the jazz guitar students he now had in the digital era were significantly different from the students he'd taught before:

> I don't think students will go back a hundred percent to the old school method because that world doesn't exist anymore. There's now much easier access to incredible amounts of music.
>
> But it's a double-edged sword, because when I was learning you had to go out to a music store to buy an object. You could hear it on the radio, maybe, but then you'd go buy this thing called an 'album' which was like 12 by 12 inches. It had album art on it and very legible liner notes on the back. You might buy two of those in a week, maybe.
>
> So you'd take it home and you'd have this one Jimi Hendrix record and you'd listen to it and as you listened you were looking at the

cover art and reading the liner notes. CDs are so small the art work loses all its pizzazz, and unless you have really good eyesight and good lighting you can't read the liner notes. Pass that little booklet around at a party? Forget it.

But look at today: You have an iPod with 64 gigabytes that can hold 30,000 albums, and however much it holds, it doesn't weigh any more. That fascinates me. Now try lugging around 30,000 LPs!

The students today already have so much on their tiny little iPods or phones that they don't know what to listen to anymore. You've listened to 30,000 records, but what have you retained? Has all that music given you more pleasure than someone had back in 1968 who played Sergeant Pepper over and over again and was just awestruck?

On the other hand I think that today those students who are meant to become the better musicians will by the nature of things go through a period of what I just described but will later focus in on what they love, trying to absorb it and make it their own.

Students fall in love with something. And of course when you're young you fall in love with something every two weeks because you're discovering all the time. They think, 'Since I love it, this is what I want to do now.' But I try to teach them that you can love something without having to do it. You have to choose something, at least for the short term and even better for the long term.

— Michael Gauthier, interview 2019

Once again, the more things change, the more they stay the same.

Instrument of change

When I brought up the topic of "scenes" in my 2017 phone interview with jazz bassist Christian McBride, he had just as much trouble as anyone identifying "the next big thing." But there was no doubt about jazz being a living, moving, shaping force in his life. Zeitgeist of the age or not, McBride loved jazz, believed in it, shared it, and used it as an instrument of positive social change.

He remarked that Wynton Marsalis, one of his mentors, had asserted that for a musician there was value in concentrating on a narrow window of jazz history:

One of the great controversies of Wynton's rise in the eighties was his seemingly narrow scope of what jazz was. He was very much not a fan of fusion. He was very much not a fan of avant-garde. Us players in our teens, we were listening to those records of Miles Davis from the eighties, and Wynton was against that. He was like, 'Put that crap away and listen to Miles from the fifties!'

While I didn't agree with that then any more than I do now, I knew that if I were to concentrate on a particular area of jazz that could help me develop as a musician while still making my secondary goal to stay on top of current trends and learn different styles of music, that would only make me a better musician.

McBride agreed with my view on the current availability of all music, pointing to the internet as both an obstacle and an opportunity for jazz musicians:

> Now that everyone has the ability to listen to any kind of music anywhere, at any time, there's no excuse for aesthetic ignorance, there's absolutely no reason why a person can't have at least a pedestrian knowledge of any form of music, and if not, it just means they choose not to look for it. Sadly, I think that the more convenient things are the less people actually take advantage of that convenience, or they take it for granted.

McBride's passion for the music manifests in his own playing, in collaborations, in his podcasts, and in the work he's done with Jazz House Kids,[16] the amazing school in New Jersey founded by his wife, Canadian singer Melissa Walker. Jazz House Kids provides a holistic musical environment for jazz excellence, recruiting many big names in jazz to provide young people of all backgrounds with a jazz environment that not only helps them grow as musicians but also instils self-confidence, self-discipline, community values, and positive personal directions.

It's doubtful that all these kids will have lived through the same depths of pain that inspired the work of geniuses like Louis Armstrong, but they are the heirs of a monumental musical tradition along with its

---

16 https://jazzhousekids.org/

henchman — cool. Some of these students will continue to keep jazz alive to the end of their days. Others will use jazz as a launching pad to other musical horizons. In some way both groups will be asked to respond somehow to the tremendous suffering in our world today, but no one will ask them to pretend everything is fine.

Cool will always be with us. The pain of the American black experience was so profound that the stance it engendered was refined by fire and alloyed with empowering metals. Jazz without cool may go on existing as an artifact, but jazz that holds onto cool can only die with music itself.

British ex-pat Graham George, who'd witnessed the metamorphosis from the fanciful Band of Joy to the full-fledged Led Zeppelin at Whiskey a Go Go in London, shared a rather dark view of how music has changed in the new millennium and a cogent argument for why initiatives like Jazz House Kids are so necessary:

> Just about anybody can create music these days, a computer and a music program with virtual instruments, and you're off! Whether you have an ear to do so, is another thing, and musicians will know if you do or not.
>
> The lack of teaching music at school in the majority of countries these days is one of the problems too. If you have a listening audience that merely requires a recognisable 'beats per minute' to dance to, with no knowledge that musically it has little meaning or needs little musicality, then the chance for good music to survive is made more difficult.
>
> —Graham George, interview 2018

Jazz of the nations

I'm always surprised at how jazz remains jazz even after taking on multiple influences on its route around the globe. I'm also surprised at how people still have a hard time grasping that this is a normal part of musical development.

Dutch guitarist Jan Wouter Oostenrijk gave me the following viewpoint:

There will always be music fans that will complain about the mixing of genres, quickly resigning musical syncretism to the realm of lesser music, music of questionable quality insofar as it represents a collage of musical styles and languages.

— Jan Wouter Oostenrijk, interview 2011

Oostenrijk is keenly aware of the creative stimulus afforded by musical crossovers. With degrees in both classical and jazz guitar (he's also studied flamenco music and Arabic melody) and with the support of an amazing band of conservatory-trained virtuosos and brilliant self-taught Moroccans, Oostenrijk has been weaving North African music into his jazz and blues performances for years, creating a rich and spicy goulash.

It hasn't always been an easy fit. "Incorporating Maghreb sounds into the musical context of jazz," he admitted, "is a never-ending puzzle. It's like integration itself, finding ways to meet and seeing what works and what doesn't. It's like learning a new language."

The spirit of music is such that it continuously transforms itself, whether or not we're ready.

A new romanticism

The world is too much with us; late and soon,
Getting and spending, we lay waste our powers;–
Little we see in Nature that is ours;
We have given our hearts away, a sordid boon!
— William Wordsworth, from the sonnet
"The World is Too Much With Us"

Wordsworth might well have been describing the malady of the present age, in which our human ills are, thanks to the information revolution, even more present to us than they were in 1802, when this sonnet was written.

The musical response to the griefs of the late eighteenth and early to late nineteenth centuries was romanticism. Operas, concertos, symphonies, and songs were preoccupied with nature, death, love, feelings, imagination, social injustice, and mythology. Romanticism in music may best have been manifested in the music of Beethoven – rich, passionate, and ingenious, inspired by folk tunes, myths, and political ideals.

The first and second world wars, the Great Depression, labour struggles, civil rights abuses, Vietnam, and the Cold War all seemed to inspire experiments in discord, silence, minor keys, novel scales, and abrasive instrumentation. Even the more accessible composers like Ravel, Satie, and Debussy weren't exactly producing happy little ditties. This wasn't music that wanted to be your friend; it was serious and demanded to be taken seriously.

The task of cheering people up, distracting them from their sorrows, and healing their traumas thus fell to popular music, which, as I've already mentioned, was mostly American jazz.

Jump ahead to the early 21st century and things are quite different. Because the little-known Kellogg-Briand pact of 1928 essentially made military conquest for its own sake illegal, the motivations behind power struggles have changed, the impetus most often religious or ideological but no less deadly.

The difference between our experience and that of our forebears is that we can't get away from the suffering of our fellow humans. We can't simply live our lives independent of the horrors taking place the world over. We have to know everything while it's happening, despite the fact that we can't do much to help. Our systems haven't evolved to the point where such knowledge leaves us unscathed.

That is, *some* of us can't get away from this knowledge; there are among us those who've chosen a comfortable little paradigm from behind which to experience life. It's rather an outdated mindset but tremendously useful in the current political climate: the assumption of an inherent superiority based on class, religion, race, gender, or all of the above.

The world is becoming increasingly polarized between two groups in a tug-of-war that will probably end up breaking the rope, sending both sides hurtling backwards into heaps.

In the first group are those who cling to the belief that they and those in their circle are the good ones; the "others" are evil and the only way to be safe from evil is to get those others as far away from us as possible, to control their activities, and to exclude them from pursuits that might grant them power. Any attempt to hold this group responsible for their own sins gets deflected into a blaming of "the other." It works: Their worldview is an effective antidote against mental and emotional distress.

In the second group are those who believe good and evil can be found everywhere and that it's up to them to boost the good and quash the evil. They hold themselves accountable for the harms perpetrated in the world around them and take steps to reverse the damage. They believe it's their duty to know what hurt is being inflicted in the world today and to stand with those who suffer. This group, more often than is healthy, forces itself to face evil. Monstrous evil. Evil that can't be destroyed, that won't go away. They're driven to listen to horrifying confessions, to view images designed to disturb them to the point of their emotional collapse. They're either trying to fix things or they're burned out from trying, and they couldn't escape if they wanted to. The info-tech era renders all this a thousand times more brutal, and people no longer need to go to war to get PTSD.

These two groups may have always existed, but the nature of politics in the world today is such that there's an enmity between them, and that enmity is growing.

Add to this the current epidemic of underserved mental health crises – which may or may not correlate with the traumatic nature of life in the 21st century – and you have a culture that reaches out to music not for intellectual stimulation, but to relieve the pain of those who remain conscious. Why? Because it works and has few side effects, and also because music was never meant to be kept separate from human concern.

> Your joy is your sorrow unmasked.
> And the selfsame well from which your laughter rises was oftentimes filled with your tears.
> And how else can it be?
> The deeper that sorrow carves into your being, the more joy you can contain.
> — *The Prophet* by Khalil Gibran

"If an artist does his art with his own sensibility," says Blaise Caillet of Swiss glitch-jazz band SKNAIL, "and this sensibility is touched by the suffering in the world, or by other global and human problems, this will be reflected in his work. That's what I feel and I try to do."

Musical syncretists tend to come from the conscious group, if only because they're more open to joining forces with "the other." Because of this, music has had to change to accommodate the depths of their pain. This is why much of the music in the first two decades of the new millennium has been neo-romantic in style and in the values it professes.

This 21st century neo-romanticism is different from the romantic revival of the sixties, with its idealistic love of nature, freedom, and social justice; today's neo-romanticism is necessarily less naïve. Music has become less a rhapsodic flight of fancy and more an effort to reveal this light within and come to an understanding with it.

Our 21st century neo-romanticism is even further removed from the 18th century version because it lacks, well – *romance*.

When I told a baby boomer acquaintance I was writing a book about how music had changed in the new millennium she blurted, "I know how! It's not as romantic!" She went on to say how much she missed the crooners, the slow dancing, and the swelling strings. "Young people today know nothing of romance."

I had to admit there was some truth in what she was saying. I have a sinking sadness when noting what was lost during the sexual revolution, mainly the agony of love's ecstasy that came with the repressive sexual mores of yesteryear. The young today will never know what that was like unless they're born into one of those increasingly rare cultures that manages to ensure couples are virgins on their wedding nights. The sweetness of a forbidden love was not only exquisite, making activities like slow dancing together almost euphoric, it kept many from experiencing a series of crushing disappointments. And it's getting harder and harder to find young people who have the expectation that one day a great love will sweep them off their feet.

Huxley's *Brave New World* suggested a time would come when unfettered sexual activity would be the norm despite indications that human beings may not be physically or emotionally fit for serial promiscuity, and it seems perhaps that that time has come.

The digital age has taken it one step further by sucking the joy out of real sexual experience. The ubiquitous presence of pornography as close as the smartphone is making many young people grow up preferring self-pleasure to couplehood, losing their physical capacity for in-person lovemaking.

This decay of conventional romance has a thin silver lining that may be leading us toward a new understanding of healthy romantic love. Current marital therapies are more and more advocating less emotional fusion between partners and more mutual respect for each other as separate individuals. This appears to be improving marriages. It took a while, but the world has finally come around to accepting Rilke's wisdom:

> The point of marriage is not to create a quick commonality by tearing down all boundaries; on the contrary, a good marriage is one in which each partner appoints the other to be the guardian of his solitude, and thus they show each other the greatest possible trust. A merging of two people is an impossibility, and where it seems to exist, it is a hemming-in, a mutual consent that robs one party or both parties of their fullest freedom and development.
> —Rainer Maria Rilke in *Letters to a Young Poet*, 1908

A new romanticism? In a relationship in which two beings are the guardians of each others' solitude one could imagine lovemaking to the music of Ludovico Einaudi, Dinuk Wijeratne, Ólafur Arnalds, Suzie LeBlanc, Christos Hatzis, or Jeff Reilly, whose compositions seem to support a deeper instrospection, a desire to know the true self – and thus true unity.

Composers like Stefano Scodanibbio, David Lang, Luciano Berio, and Missy Mazzoli write ample dissonance into their pieces, but their themes are nearly always romantic. Music by composers of the romantic era resonates far more now than forty years ago. Missy Mazzoli experienced this sense of connection with the romantics when first discovering Beethoven:

> There wasn't any classical music in my environment, but we happened to have a piano my parents bought at a flea market. I discovered Beethoven early on through a piano teacher, and devoured every recording of his works I could find. It felt random and chaotic, but I treasured every piece by Beethoven that I heard. Each musical discovery felt like it was mine alone.
> —Missy Mazzoli, interview 2013

Mazzoli wrote *Song from the Uproar,* an opera based on the life and writings of Isabelle Eberhardt, an eccentric 19th-century Swiss aristocrat who moved to Algeria and converted to Islam. You'd be hard-pressed to find a more romantic heroine, her life a search for freedom, love, and epiphany. Says Mazzoli:

> I feel that Isabelle Eberhardt's struggles mirror those of many people, particularly women, in the 21st century. She finds herself caught between her need to lead an independent life and her desire to settle down with her husband. She also struggles to express herself in an often hostile environment. Ultimately her story is about discovering and remaining faithful to one's true self in the face of extreme loneliness and adversity.

This preoccupation with the true self could never have become what it is today without 20th century psychoanalytical writings that challenged the dominance of existentialist philosophy. It's through this lens of the concept of the true self that we've revisited the literature of the past, looking for examples of those who've managed to peel back the layers of social morality, manifest personality, and conformity to encounter and embrace the light within themselves.

According to Dinuk Wijeratne escapism and realism are partners in the quest for meaning:

> Daniel Barenboim is my favourite musical philosopher and his big credo is that music is a metaphor for life. I believe absolutely in that; music is the perfect tool for understanding yourself and the world, not in terms of specific events but in terms of how human beings function in society and in themselves. It's escapism and also a window to understanding.
> — Dinuk Wijeratne, interview 2010

The compositions of Christos Hatzis changed in response to his own journey of self-understanding, becoming more spiritual:

> I think that our most profound creativity springs from the need to balance an imbalanced environment. At least this is how it was in

the beginning. Later, when spirituality became an important ingredient of who I am and what kind of music I write, my music became a kind of 'prayer in sound,' so it is now only possible to compose in a prayerful state of mind.

— Christos Hatzis, interview 2010

Jeff Reilly sees composition as a deeply rewarding form of play:

People often forget that music is actually like a sophisticated game plan. There are no winners or losers, but you're really playing a game; and the better you play the game, the more fun you have, the kind of fun that provides a deep, heartfelt, complex human satisfaction.

— Jeff Reilly, interview 2010

My own obsession with music was still driven by curiosity but also by an urge to seek refuge from my pain the way I always had – by letting music be my refuge, looking to it to give me that "deep, heartfelt, complex human satisfaction" that was the only real antidote to my misery.

My snooty teenaged self would have scoffed at the idea of seeking out music that soothed and comforted, which was tantamount to choosing music as escape. My music was chosen for its power to exhort, challenge, solidify, motivate, or at the very least to enhance the intellectual mystique I was trying to cultivate. Little did I know how this flew in the face of what music is.

My eventual acceptance of ambient and meditation music was a response to punishing life circumstances that I couldn't allow to cripple me. I now see that surrendering to this mindset, giving up my pride that is, was part of music's agenda.

Ambient, new age, meditation music, and, the most musically sophisticated form of all of these, jazz fusion, have the power to relax, to calm, to uplift, and best of all, to reassure you that it's still mostly a beautiful world. And they're all, I think it's safe to say, products of the postmodern world even though their roots run much deeper. I often listen to these genres while working, to reduce my stress levels and help me concentrate. The music may be strange at times but isn't meant to monopolize my attention. The sounds are often similar to those found in nature, so working along with them is like working beside a bubbling mountain stream with birds singing all around.

In these last two decades ambient music has come into its own, providing therapy, replacing muzak, and serving as background music in massage rooms all over the world. And its continuing development appears to be just as natural and organic as the process of listening.

Even if you turn up your nose at the thought of music as something to ease suffering or heal the sick, knowing that it's not an ideal world means that at the very least music will be called upon to reassure us of the value of existence.

> Music helps you to digest what happens to you, what you live. When two people look at the same piece of art they see different things because they make sense of different parts, or they take a different angle on it. The work is 50 percent creator and 50 percent spectator. Like when you have a breakup you listen to sad songs because it helps you make sense of what you've lived. It helps you grieve. It's a catalyst of human experience.
>
> — Alex Cégé, lead singer of Mangeur de Rêves, interview 2019

"The day the music died"

The release of the song "American Pie" by Don McLean in 1971 was a singular event in rock history, mainly because it provided such an accurate example of the historical pattern peculiar to music in general and to rock music in particular.

It's common knowledge that the song's oft-repeated phrase, "the day the music died," refers to the day in 1959 on which three rock and roll luminaries, Buddy Holly ("Peggy Sue"), J.P. Richardson ("Chantilly Lace"), and Richie Valens ("La Bamba") and their pilot met their fates in a plane that crashed near Clear Lake, Iowa.

Watch an old video of Buddy Holly and the Crickets on the Ed Sullivan and you'll be struck by the contrast between early rockers – nice southern boys who listened to their mothers' admonition to act polite and dress neat — and the long-haired rabble rousers that were to come. You might also notice the condescending manner Sullivan betrays when introducing "these Texas boys," something you don't see in his slightly nervous introductions of the Rolling Stones.

At first music managers insisted that the performers they represented be genteel and clean-cut, but all that went out the window when they realized that more money could be made with disheveled, disreputable bohemian types.

On New Year's Eve 1972 I was glued to my radio as "American Pie" climbed to song of the year on the hit parade. This song *mattered*. Even before I knew the history behind it I knew "American Pie" pointed to a rock tragedy. It had taken Don McLean 12 years to come to terms with the event of 1959 and use it as a catalyst for an anthem to lost innocence.

In this 12 years Western culture had changed irrevocably. It had climbed to an idealistic mountaintop and thrown itself off it. It had torn down edifices and rebuilt them. It had returned to the garden and left it littered with roaches and needles. It had preached free love and practiced insensitive sexual exploitation. All that had once seemed solid and permanent was now doubted and challenged.

On so many levels this cultural disruption had to happen, and it certainly wasn't the first period of social upheaval in history. Besides, there were many positive outcomes – movements of peaceful resistance and a search for spiritual meaning, for example – that came out of this questioning of past practices. But the chaos of the sixties left many wondering how to cope in this new world.

I asked my father what it had been like to grow up in America in the staid forties and fifties and then to go through the turbulent sixties as a young father.

"It didn't strike me as so strange when I was going through it," he said, "but some time in the early seventies I looked around and realized everything had changed. People no longer had to get married. They didn't have to stay married. It was no longer necessary to get your hair cut and dress neatly. No one respected authority anymore. All the tastes and values were different."

The sixties made popular music more political and more experimental, and some used it to replicate what people experienced while experimenting with mind-altering substances. The sixties was a neo-romantic musical era, fixated on love, nature, freedom, and defiance of injustice.

Don McLean wrote "American Pie" in 1971, so my father hadn't been the only one suffering an existential crisis. McLean had recognized that with all that had been gained a purity had been lost.

The existential experiments might have had more positive outcomes had they not been accompanied by so much self-righteousness. The sixties had brought in an oppositional mindset leading to a descent into immorality every bit as nasty as the bourgeois decadence the young had castigated. Again, this was in part due to record industry marketers who saw in the misbehaviour of young musicians a shock factor that guaranteed higher profits. Teenaged fans liked seeing their idols act up in ways they couldn't, not only getting away with it but rewarded for it with posh lifestyles.

I remember how this felt as a child. The television musical extravaganzas I'd once been glued to lost their sheen for me as I realized they were "square." I was learning to see this whole era as no more than escapist fluff; my generation, or rather the generation I hoped to join, was going to be better than that. Why? Because it had adopted a natural look and loved folk music and rock. Because it hated war. Because it wore paisley and did macramé. Because it refused to eat canned peas. Because it wasn't materialistic. Because it was young.

All of this was but a veil over the truth. McLean made the plane crash a historical dividing line between innocent joys and the narcissistic psychopathy into which rock musicians and their fans had descended.

All the promising catch phrases eventually rang hollow. Free love turned out to be just another patriarchal power ploy, as Joni Mitchell pointed out years later. Today's older feminists credit the birth of their consciousness-raising to the contempt with which they were treated during the "revolutionary" experiments of the sixties. Recently Marianne Faithful, Mick Jagger's early muse and a poster child for female sexual freedom, admitted that until the age of 50 she hadn't been able to make love without being drunk or high. Linda Lovelace revealed that in the film *Deep Throat* we were actually witnessing her rape.

So much for love. As for peace, well, as John Lennon showed us, if someone rubbed you the wrong way you didn't really have to give it a chance.

Still the media promoted the flower power generation as pure and innocent and at the same time wild and free, throwing traditional morality to the winds. It had already happened in jazz, and as the country music industry began to burgeon in the forties and fifties executives noticed that the more the cowboy yodellers sang about cheatin', drinkin', and divorcin',' the more sales went up, which was kind of weird considering how prudish country folks tend to be. It's how country music morphed from exhortatory rural songs to the lower-than-a-snake's belly downer much of it sank to later on.

Rap and hip hop, which showed so much creative promise in their beginnings and which still occasionally flash with brilliance, quickly became layered down in the trappings of a carefully constructed fantasy of urban life.

Singer-songwriter Emay Holmes is a cultivated young African American steeped in the poetry of Hafiz, Rumi, Neruda, and Bukowski, but he'd felt pressure as a musician to conform to someone else's idea of what his life should be:

> I used to rap about clothes and cars and women even though I was in a place in my life where none of that was true. I was talking about all the stuff I didn't have. Many people do that and it doesn't hurt their conscience, but for me I could put out dishonest music for only so long. It wasn't genuine. I was a lot more comfortable with rapping when I focused on my own issues.
>
> — Emay Holmes, interview 2018

Record executives also turned a blind eye and may at times have been complicit in their charges being continuously plied with alcohol and illicit drugs. Young musicians are just as prone as any youth to feeling invincible, and many simply didn't know what they were taking. Need more pep for your tour? Take this. Trouble sleeping? Here you go. Wanna party? Have I got something for you . . .

Singer Fabiola Cacciatore told me that when she fronted a band in the eighties fans would line the front of the stage with drinks, and she'd often shake hands with strangers to come away with a handful of pills. It was considered a form of worship, the offering of libations to an idol. It was also a a way for dealers to develop a network of rich clientele.

We didn't have to lose Amy Winehouse to know how deeply this went against the spirit of music itself. And we didn't have to lose Holly,

Valens, and Richardson to acknowledge that comfortable executives were forcing keen musicians, ready to accept any hardship to further their careers, to travel in unheated buses until they became so ill they had to hire planes at their own expense.

It took decades for the widespread resentment and disappointment in the music industry to build to a point where it would fuel today's DIY movement, but when the technology was ready, so were the musicians.

Perhaps a further disappointment might revive the custom of ordinary people gathering to make music together.

Marty Night

One thing I noticed about the rise of recorded music in general was that bit by bit it had edged out the common practice of making music at home. Recordings in my lifetime were so trimmed and polished that we got used to perfection, and it spoiled us. It wasn't so easy to listen to Grandpa sawing away on the fiddle or Dad squeezing out a tune on the harmonica, and now when we sang it somehow mattered that we were off-key and couldn't remember all the words.

I watched as families that normally sang and played instruments together slowly went off to separate rooms and turned to the television, radio, or record player to amuse themselves in the evenings. Performance became more and more the pastime of musical elites. Families and friends who saw themselves as having talent would get together to make music in the hope that some day they might be discovered by the music industry. There was less playing for the joy of it, for the good of your soul; the music industry was always hovering close by. It was on people's minds, and few of us could think about music without it.

My parents had grown up with plenty of live music but were loathe to listen to their music-loving children practice. It was easier for my extrovert brothers to get past this than it was for me; I'd always assumed that much as I loved music I lacked any musical gifts worth sharing with others. I also had the kind of personality that shrank from appearing before groups of people. For me music became a private pastime, a shutting of doors to softly pluck and sing as I studied my tablatures.

I must repeat that I don't think of recorded music as a negative force to be battled. It's one of many ways to make and listen to music – just not the only way.

In spite of myself I eventually began singing and playing my guitar and banjo with other musicians. I learned that there's something transcendent about playing music yourself, listening to the musicians around you, adjusting your volume and tempo to theirs, improvising, feeding off their bliss or hearing them feed off yours. Given enough freedom and encouragement, even amateur groups can generate moments of celestial harmony that can never be repeated. It's the po' folks' version of the audiophile experiment Cowley had talked about.

We had to be willing to sound awful until we could get to sounding good, and not everyone has this kind of patience; it takes a special courage and perseverance to get to sounding good. But just playing music with other musicians, when it's not pressured by demands for perfection, is the kind of feel-good communication that restores connection. Even when few words are exchanged you can have soul-opening conversations with music. You may not know quite what you said to each other, but you know that the dialogue affirmed both of you, making you a part of something grand.

In 2011 I said good-bye to the Dixie Hicks and the Radio Stardust Jazz Orchestra and brought my Labrador retriever, banjo, and guitar down to New Hampshire to stay with my brother Ben, his wife Stephanie, and their then three children.

It was Ben who came up with the idea of inviting a few friends over once a week for a music jam. One couple, Fritz and Kris, had a son named Marty who was around the same age as Ben's boys, and it tickled them pink that Marty was to come over every week and play with them while the grownups hootenannied. That's how the event came to be known as Marty Night.

We didn't care how we sounded, but when we sounded good we were especially happy and when we sounded terrible we had a good laugh. We played and sang mostly folk and classic rock, but we also did jazz standards, world music, hymns, old tymey, and bluegrass. We threw in a few surprises, like "Brand New Best Friend" from the cartoon *Phineas and Ferb*, the *Bonanza* theme song, and some very weird songs brought to us by Viola Dutton, a goldmine of strange old tunes (e.g. "The Little Blue Man," by Betsy Johnson).

Every week someone would say, "Hey, could we do this one?" and somebody would later look up the song with its chords and print it off to hand out for the next week. We all kept song binders, and sometimes there were long delays between songs as people tried to find the right sheet. We would break to snack on home-baked goodies and sip herbal tea or craft beer. The children played raucously in the next room under the vigilant eye of Stephanie, my patient sister-in-law. They rarely joined us, but we knew we were giving them invaluable memories, a model of adult interaction to which they one day would (we hoped) return.

The song we'd always close off with was *"Die Gedanken sind Frei"* ("The Mind is Free"). This song had first started appearing on German broadsides as early as 1780, but the origins of the song may predate that by centuries. In the last century it was publicly performed and recorded by the Weavers, Pete Seeger, Leonard Cohen, the Limeliters, and a host of other folksingers, and I recently saw a wonderful punk German version of it on a Youtube video.

And then there was us, the Marty Night crew. We roared out as we sang:

> Die gedanken sind frei –
> This thought gives me pleasure.
> My conscience decrees, this right I must treasure.
> My thoughts will not cater
> To duke or dictator
> No one can deny –
> Die gedanken sind frei!

We were a gang of Christians, agnostics, atheists, and pagans, and we were revelling in the one thing we could all agree on: our minds were *free!* Outside this living room were people whose gun-totin' political rants left us feeling raw, but there together we had a sweet solidarity. No matter what came, we took pleasure in thinking as we pleased. It might take a little work to help scrape away the blinding muck of propaganda flung at us from all directions, but if we wanted to find the meaning in things, we could. It was there for us, because the song said so and because we'd sung it together. It was a mutual affirmation.

Marty Night, if it had happened in the 20th century, wouldn't have stood out as anything particularly special, but in this age of musical isolationism it was a rare and poignant reminder that life is beautiful just the way it is and that connecting with others through music is a grand privilege.

Rise up, go home, and sing!

The Occupy movement began in 2011 in response to a feature in the Canadian activist magazine *Adbusters*. The publication called on readers to occupy Wall Street to protest the way the power of banks and other corporate bodies had engineered a shocking degree of economic inequality.

That's all it took: somebody saying, "Hey people, go out and march. Occupy public spaces. Show your opposition, and speak truth to power!"

But such calls to action are based on the "us and them" mentality of those who think fighting evil means beating whoever we believe to be the bad guys.

The call I'm about to make to you now doesn't assume that you or I are better than anyone else or any less responsible for the quagmire of corruption and injustice the world keeps sinking into. But neither does it assume we're all fundamentally evil and have to keep beating ourselves up over things we have no power to change. The one thing that most of us can agree on is that we're nearly all suffering in some way or other, and if we're blessed with peace and plenty we need to have a little compassion for those who aren't.

Certain members of the music industry have actually done a tremendous amount of good while others have thrown artists to the curb and sold us a landfill of bad music. The music industry isn't bad, it's just there. We need it, in fact. But should the music industry crowd all music out of our lives except for the music they're trying to sell us?

My call to you is to occupy music. Learn an instrument. Sing. They'll get used to the rough bits — you'll see. Don't cave to the weaknesses of others; what you're doing is important. Write songs and make people listen to them. Go on enjoying radio, television, and mp3s, and go on singing songs recorded by other people, but make your own music, alone and in company. I want to see a world full of Marty Nights. Let's make it happen. This will be our response to the pain in the world, and our attempt to heal it in a small way. The planet will thank us.

It plays us

I had an extremely slow dawning insight about creation. That insight is that context largely determines what is written, painted, sculpted, sung, or performed. That doesn't sound like much of an insight, but it's actually the opposite of conventional wisdom, which maintains that creation emerges out of some interior emotion, from an upwelling of passion or feeling.

—David Byrne, in *How Music Works*, 2012

Byrne's statement suggests that creation is in part a process transcending the individual. If you're a creative person and observe yourself as a phrase enters your head and then writes itself into a poem, or a tune enter yours head to bloom into a song, or an image enters your head that longs to be a painting, you may have the sense that inspiration is somehow bigger than you are, arriving from somewhere else.

But of course this is an illusion, because creation doesn't emerge from any physical location. It can no more be said to spring from our environments than it can be said to spring from our hearts or our instruments. The sense that it's somehow in sync with both our hearts and our contexts doesn't prove a thing. Music, for example, has no place, and this alone is sufficient testimony to its spiritual essence. It's there, and it plays us.

I've often drawn correlations between political climates and the musical genres that prevail during their lifespans, pointing out that that punk rock re-emerges during periods of political conservatism, particularly when the gap widens between the powerful and the powerless.

Neo-romantic music expresses our widespread longing to return to nature, to romantic love, to the ideals of social justice, simplicity, and freedom of emotion and expression. So naturally neo-romantic music emerges during eras when those things are most threatened.

But let's not stop there. What about the jubilant lightheartedness of early jazz as a mighty attempt to rise above the shocking displays of racial hatred African Americans couldn't escape? What about the rise of sixties psychedelic rock and the simultaneous disenchantment with authority figures? What about folk music as human integrity pushing back against class oppression?

Why is it that when a civilization moves in one direction music chooses to move in another?

Music reacts, refuses, gets its heels down, and rants, and it's certainly a channelling of the universal wounded child begging for release and healing, but music is also a shrieking canary alerting us to the presence of gas in the coal mine, an interpretive dancer showing us the true meanings hidden in the events of our passing days, a teenager struggling toward a personal identity by insisting they're not like their parents. Music answers our existential hunger, sometimes railing against those who've made off with our existential food.

Music's courtroom

My aim was in part to try to answer the question, *What is so different about the music of the first two decades of the new millennium?*

I repeat, for one, that every genre that has ever existed is now speaking to us at once. Technology has opened the door to voices we'd never have heard before, voices finally united to speak against authority, greed, religious fundamentalism, sexism, racism, and class oppression and to create social conditions that promote healing, change, and true progress — the construction of meaningful lives.

These days there's no dominant voice monopolizing our attention, and that's what makes us postmodern. We're standing in music's courtroom, and the powers that be are on trial.

Are they listening?

The Mindful Bard

By 2005 I'd worked out a personal mission statement that I felt rose above the conventional conflict between artistic and social obligations:

> To cultivate within myself mindfulness, compassion, and diligence in order to free myself to create art as a natural response to suffering.

This didn't mean getting up on a soapbox, but it might on occasion have led to that. It didn't always mean being serious, although sometimes it was. Sometimes it meant just making people laugh good and hard or thrilling them with beauty or delighting them with some new idea or granting them respite from their pain. Sometimes it meant opening people's minds. Sometimes it meant challenging authority and inviting others to do the same.

I'd come to believe that wholehearted art, mindful art, that is, the best art, naturally responded to suffering, regardless of the maker's intention. When art deliberately ceases to block this process, either by forcing a specific charitable action or by refusing to perform it, culture suffers. An artist's refusal to respond with compassion to human pain will not in itself lead to horrific events, which come from complex conditions, but art has a role to play in preventing war and genocide. Art can't be separated from suffering any more than it can be separated from joy. This is especially true of music.

I applied this mission statement as a standard against which to judge new music. Many of the musical works I chose to write about didn't in any way encourage compassion, but neither did they discourage it, and they had so much of that special something that they empowered me to write and sing better. Some just provided a rejuvenating break. Some artists openly pursued specific social objectives, like Jazz House Kids, or Conjunto Rocque Moreira's aiding of poor Brazilian children, or Preservation Hall's initiative to protect and preserve New Orleans jazz.

When I interviewed musicians and composers I had a common set of questions that I tweaked for each artist. After the normal preliminaries I would sometimes lead up to this little query:

Do you think artists should respond to the suffering in the world?

It was already, in my mind, the embryo of a long-term research project. With rare exceptions musical artists would answer this in the negative. No one wanted their art to be saddled with that kind of burden. But when I explained that a response to suffering is something that happens quite naturally in music making if you let it, most agreed that this was happening with them.

I had a list of criteria. If a piece of music (I also recommended books and films, but mostly music) fit two of these criteria, it was worth a listen. This was my criteria for a worthy piece of Mindful Bard art:

1. It's authentic, original, and delightful.
2. It poses and admirably responds to questions that have a direct bearing on my view of existence.
3. It stimulates my mind.
4. It harmoniously unites art with social action, saving me from both seclusion in an ivory tower and slavery to someone else's political agenda.
5. It provides respite from a sick and cruel world, a respite enabling me to renew myself for a return to mindful artistic endeavor.
6. It's about attainment of the true self.
7. It inspires an awareness of the sanctity of creation.
8. It makes me want to be a better artist.
9. It gives me tools of compassion, enabling me to respond with love and efficacy to the suffering around me.
10. It renews my enthusiasm for positive social action.
11. It makes me appreciate that life is a complex and rare phenomena, making living a unique opportunity (suggested by Cybiont).

Though initially Darryl Klassen resisted the idea that art should carry a message, he did come around to acknowledging a wish that his work reflect the love in the universe:

I've always reacted strongly to the view that the arts are compelled somehow to convey a message. We don't expect carpenters to build only hospitals or churches, or mechanics to fix only school buses or ambulances. A song, a poem, or a painting stands on its own and should be judged accordingly.

Authentic songs originate somehow in one's own experience . . . I am a disciple of Jesus. I'm not a very good one, and I'm sure as hell not very religious, but I think we live in a created, orderly universe. There is an invisible realm that surrounds us – call it spiritual if you want – and it's somehow more important than this visible one. Its primary characteristic is love.

— Darryl Klassen of J.D. Miner, interview 2016

Marc Vella, the French classical pianist and composer, allowed his natural compassion to rise and bubble over into a beautiful adventure, travelling with a baby grand piano across more than forty countries, giving impromptu performances and inviting local musicians to join him. His mission was to share love and to celebrate humanity as part of the International Decade for the Promotion of a Culture of Peace and Non-Violence for the Children of the World, coordinated by UNESCO.

When in 2014, during his tour of villages in the Maghreb, I asked Vella what was next for him, he wrote: "*Au travail ! Il y a des hommes à transformer vers l'amour.*" (To work! There are men to transform towards love.)

When I asked him what he'd learned from other musicians en route he said, "*C'est simple, je n'écris plus aujourd'hui. Comme eux, j'improvise. Ce lien avec l'instant présent est essentiel. Il permet à la grâce (l'inspiration) de se manifester. Se laisser la traverser est une expérience extatique considérable.*" ("It's simple – I do not write today. Like them, I improvise. This connection with the present moment is essential. It allows grace [inspiration] to manifest itself. To let oneself go through it is an ecstatic experience.")

When in 2013 I asked Cameroon guitarist Jack Djeyim about his beliefs he wrote, "*Mes idéologies et ma religion, c'est 'l'amour et le partage!'*" ("My ideology and religion are 'love and sharing!'")

Many of the musicians I interviewed subscribed to a low-key religiosity or none at all, but it wasn't just Vella, Klassen, and Djeyim who professed love as their religion.

Bringing in Voice

In 2013 I had the privilege of being accompanied by the Michael Gauthier Trio, at 100,000 Poets for Change in Montreal. The poems I read to the packed room had been published online and on paper, but I'd never seen evidence that anyone had read them besides the editors. For years I'd felt like I'd almost have to pay people to read my poems, and passing them to friends nearly always resulted in no comment. Telling people I wrote poetry was a good way to get them to change the subject. But reading these same poems out loud to musical accompaniment went over like free beer.

I should have heeded the wake-up call back when I'd read my poems at the Sister Fair in Bridgetown, but opportunities for spoken art were few and far between in Nova Scotia. I was in Montreal now, so I had no excuse. I thought of putting another band together and hitting the cafés, but I'd already bought my plane ticket for Tunisia, where my music and poetry were to be put on hold for the next two years. I could still write, of course, so the Mindful Bard went on.

As a digital nomad I had at least a little money trickling in each month in return for work I was able to conduct in the comfort of my home, on my own time, wherever I lived. But as more people were landing on the gig planet it became harder to find clients, and the pay was dropping, even for experienced professionals. Two of my best clients cut back my work just before we returned to Canada, so life was a mad scramble for both Ahmed and I to find jobs as soon as we landed. I continued writing online as my French wasn't yet up to serving the public here in Montreal. Ahmed was able to find work in factories, where immigrants could usually find low-paying work until they were able to get certified in their own trades or professions.

The stresses and strains of life were piling up, and after the kind of reflection I always do when I hit an emotional impasse, I realized I needed to find somebody to jam with at least once a week. My online search led me to an ad by singer Fabiola Cacciatore, who was looking for band members to play the songs from her CD, *It's My Dream*.

She'd created the album herself with the aid of a few friends, her husband Jean de Sousa, and producer John Hagopian. I listened to the CD and liked the songs and arrangements so much that I called her up to offer my services. She invited me to her studio, which was the upstairs of her house. I sang a little, played a little, and got invited to the first rehearsal.

Though not a professional (I'd described myself as an advanced amateur) I'd had so much experience working with other musicians that I found that part easy.

Although I only stayed with the band for a little over a year I'd had enough time to develop a songwriting relationship with the lead guitarist, Gilbert Cantin. Gilbert asked me to write English lyrics for some of his compositions. I told him I'd like to try doing a song in both languages, so the first song we did together was a bluegrass song called "*Mets Ton Pantalons, Jean,*" based on the story of how my grandfather had been in the bath when he'd seen the barn catch fire and had torn out of the house in the buff to douse the flames.

Gilbert, who'd written the tune, loved it, recorded it, and put it on a couple of websites. He then introduced me to his songwriting partner, Chantal Lepage, who wrote French lyrics for his songs. We hit if off and began trading lyrics and ideas. I would translate her text, make it into verses, add my own ideas, then adapt it all either to a jazz standard chord progression or to a tune by Gilbert. I'd sing the song and send the track to Gilbert, then he'd add his own tracks and mix them.

Gilbert got busy promoting our songs. He worked much faster than I did, in spite of having fulltime work, which I rarely had, but I did scout around a little for online resources. Gilbert could write a song in the morning and have a recording of it on iTunes by nightfall, but I didn't have that kind of pluck, and I had no studio resources except for Garageband installed on my Macbook. Still, this was the direction I wanted to be headed in; the emotional rewards of songwriting were simply too great to ignore. It felt good to be feeling good again.

In my explorations I discovered Drooble, a social network for musicians. It had grown out of a musicians' cooperative in Bulgaria, the founder, Melina Krumova, having thought it worked so well it should go online and international.

The setup was brilliant – you'd create a public profile and post some songs. Anyone who liked your music could comment and anyone who saw you as a possible collaborator could get in touch. When I posted some of our basic recordings there I was amazed at the immediate response they got from the other musicians. Several composers contacted me, offering to write music. Audio engineers offered to mix my tracks for me. Musicians offered to send tracks, and songwriters invited me to sing their songs.

To top it off, the music I heard on Drooble was so good it became part of my daily listening. I found delicious jazz, experimental, folk, classical, and rock music. And I made lasting friendships. Ken Shelton of Mississippi, Christian Verhoeven of Belgium, Reynalds Leroux and Cristina Bernadat from southern France, and several others became my regular collaborators.

I could easily imagine all of my online music listening being satisfied by Drooble, and even much of my musical collaboration. It seemed strange and even a little naughty that we were making and consuming music independent of the music industry. I had to bear in mind that Drooble too was a business and might one day become a heartless corporation, but for now it felt like we'd all been shipwrecked on a magical island where we could work together to make all the music we wanted.

I no longer felt alone in my creative activities. I was still writing, but in writing songs I could be myself, explore music, and get a reaction. I now understood why I'd started to grow depressed before. Music was some kind of a pipeline for me; something came down it, I didn't know what, that gave me the will to live. And it wasn't enough just to listen – I had to be creating music as well.

I was finding more joy in music making just as I was becoming discouraged with my literary career. I'd been toiling away for a couple of years working on this book as well as several art book projects with Susan Malmstrom, who with Jack was now back in California. We'd stayed in touch and were creating works that thrilled us both all to pieces. The rejection letters were flattering: *We really like your book, but we don't know how we would market something like this*. It was disheartening, especially since we had a host of ideas waiting to be brought to life.

Whereas playing music and writing songs was uplifting and regenerating, writing prose was a long, solitary slog, leaving me feeling exhausted and alone. The dawn of information technology had connected me with people the world over while creating distance between me and the people in my physical circle. I envied 19th and 20th century writers who'd stayed up all night talking with their intellectual peers. I hadn't done that since the smartphone.

As if that wasn't enough, the material rewards of my writing just went on shrinking. I'd been paying my debts and bills by blogging, copywriting, editing, and managing social media for businesses – dull and thankless work, but it beat waitressing. Due to growing competition, compensation was diminishing. Because there was no water fountain I could go to to pick up rumours, I'd have no idea of budgetary problems until the day the client emailed me with "Sorry, but we can no longer pay you."

By November of 2018 I'd quit one client for not paying the other writers. A legal blog that had promised me regular work suddenly stopped sending assignments. A recovery blog lost a key supporter and they had to let the writers go. A charitable foundation that engaged me turned out to be no more than a tax shelter for a crooked businessman slowly succumbing to dementia.

I decided to redirect my creative energies from literature to song. I'd gotten enough positive responses and had read enough to know that I could earn a little money as a songwriter. At that point I had nothing to lose. I'd given prose my all for over a decade and it was time to throw in the towel.

That's when I received this email message from Michael Mirolla:

> Dear Wanda,
>
> I trust this finds you well.
> If your manuscript is still available, we would like to see the entire book just to be certain. But from what we've seen thus far, it is very likely we would make an offer for publication.
> All the best.
>
> Michael

This book, from which I'd taken a hiatus after the umpteenth rejection, now had to be finished. Fair enough; it would be my swan song as a writer. But it meant putting the musical projects on hold until I finished it. I told my musical friends not to expect any collaboration from me for at least four months.

I still hadn't learned my lesson. Within a week or two I became depressed; the music simply could not be put on ice. It took me three months to wake up and start playing and singing again.

I had to have music every day, not just listening but writing songs, practicing my instruments, recording, and performing with other musicians. I needed music for my mental health. But why?

In my adolescence and early adulthood I'd had a recurring dream in which I was standing on a mountainside surrounded by rolling mists and playing a flute – music so beautiful it made me shudder. I'd wake up feeling deeply moved, as if I'd been exhorted to undertake a great mission. I didn't own a flute when I dreamed that dream, but I had learned how to play one for the high school band. Later when my brother found one in a pawn shop in New York and brought it to me the dreams stopped.

I've struggled for years to discover the meaning of that dream, and today all I can say for sure is that it was a reminder that with air, an instrument, and the human body a little bit of Paradise can be brought down to earth, and that someone or something was calling me to return to my true self.

In my darkest hours I'd tried to follow M. Scott Peck's advice to look for grace. I was able to focus on the blessing of air, and used deep breathing in my meditations, along with a mantra. This was how I instilled in my heart the recognition that I was loved. I needed this. Others needed to hear it. I continued working on the book but also made time for music each day.

A presence

I must once again refer to Frye's book, *The Great Code: The Bible and Literature*, in which he explained the significance of the Bible for Western literature without taking a stance on the Bible's religious meaning — a singular mission and not without criticism from both sides of the fence.

Toward the end of the book Frye made a cryptic statement about what the Bible means for those who read it, a statement I paraphrase thus: *The Bible is a set of books which in the reading slowly allow a presence to come to the fore.*

This definition comes closest to something everyone of any religion, and even a few atheists and agnostics, might accept. It also honours the Bible's unfathomable mystery, avoiding making of it a scientific treatise, a set of malleable dogmas, or anything else it's not.

In my search for an answer to the question *What is music?* I'd found pretty much the same thing: *Music is a practice of listening and creating sound which if attended to allows a presence to slowly come to the fore.*

The older I get the less I'm inclined to define what that presence is, but the more acquainted I am with it the more I love it – and the more loved I feel.

Yes, music is mystical, and we have far more to gain from living in its sacred space than we can win from trying to make sense of the miracle of it.

In 2018 I was privileged to witness a beautiful baptism at the People's Church in downtown Montreal. We were told that the young man was autistic and also studying composition at the Boston Conservatory. Each person was invited to give their testimony of faith before they entered the baptismal tank, and this nervous, rather awkward young man, made a statement that grew ever more stirring as he went on. I will never forget his final words, delivered in a powerful voice, his hands spread open at his sides:

". . . because *God* says, *My* strength is *perfected* in *weakness!"*

Slave, exile, survivor, mystic

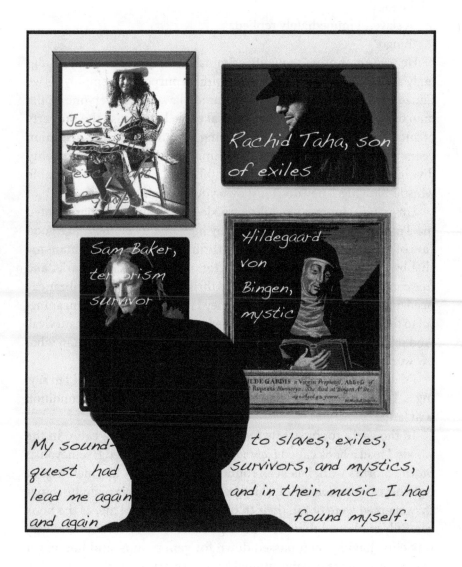

Jesse M[...]

Rachid Taha, son of exiles

Sam Baker, terrorism survivor

Hildegaard von Bingen, mystic

HILDEGARDIS a Virgin Prophetess, Abbess of Ruperts Nunnery. She died at Bingen A.º D. 1180 Aged 92 years.

My sound-quest had lead me again and again to slaves, exiles, survivors, and mystics, and in their music I had found myself.

Slave

An acquaintance of questionable character posed this question: "What do you call someone who's completely dependent on another person's money for their survival? Another person who controls their time, even off the job?"

"A slave," I immediately replied.

"Bingo."

He was attempting to justify criminal activity, but I had to grudgingly agree with his argument if not with its purpose. As employees we Canadians are still under English common law, where everyone is "the man of a man," that is, in some unshakeable legal sense the property of another. As I learned while studying labour law during my union years, you can be fired for badmouthing your boss, or for drunkenly divulging company secrets on your off time, or even for justifiable whistle-blowing. They don't just own you during paid hours.

I'm grateful for every piddling trickle-down capitalism has granted me. I'm thankful to rich folks who buy high quality clothes, take good care of them, and then give them to thrift shops so I can maintain my shabby genteel mystique. I'm grateful for posh libraries, lush parks, and free concerts. But in order to get to the thrift shops, parks, and libraries I need money, and in order to have money I must perform work meaningful to the system but pointless to me except that it enables my survival. And in order for capitalism to succeed I must be paid less than what my work is worth.

I'd never compare my existence with that of real slaves. All I'm saying is, I get it: Slavery is cruel and unjust – *and* it's the human condition writ large.

In the early 2000s, while I was still living in the log cabin in the woods, I read a book called *Lightningbolt,* by a man named Hyemeyohsts Storm. Storm's work has been roundly criticized by a few members of the Cheyenne nation, from which he's descended, for explaining things they claimed were not in their tradition. This puzzled me, as the book carefully explained that the teachings come from an ancient and very tiny elite, having been passed down for generations, and had never gained acceptance in conventional Native American spirituality within any tribe.

Storm laid out the medicine wheel teachings in careful detail, tracing them back to a small Mayan sect. I was blown sideways when he explained that these Mayans had seen the zero not as nothing, but rather as the door through which all things emerge, that is, the portal through which the spiritual becomes physical. The wheel thus becomes a symbol of the nature of things and a reminder of where these things originated.

To very briefly summarize the medicine wheel, in these teachings existence is presented as a circle divided into four quadrants. Each quadrant represents one of the four directions, one of the four elements, and one of the four sacred herbs. In the Mi'kmaq tradition with which I was familiar these herbs were sage, sweetgrass, tobacco, and cedar, which are the same herbs used in the smudging ceremony. The wheel has also been divided into four general ethnic groups, four personality types, and many other sets of categories.

The part of the teaching that stuck with me was connected with the zero idea: that all true authority rests at the round centre of the wheel, with the creator, and that not one of the quadrants was to to be valued above another. Although humans need to respect and honour other beings, we owe our highest devotion to whatever is beyond *things*. Without this teaching the heart closes, overfocussed on some narrow portion of life and blind to all others, ready to compromise what it knows to be the just path. Even the rich and powerful are in danger of becoming enslaved to materialism, substances, and other human beings. I was a slave when I chose to put my art aside because it didn't make enough money to pay for my subsistence.

Music has reminded me again and again that life is nasty, brutish, and short and that very few can escape some form of slavery or another. Music also showed me that I'm a spiritual being who can find my freedom in what lies beyond the visible.

Exile

A few years ago my mother, who'd been rooting through some old papers in the attic, showed me the deportation order made out to me when I was four years old, on the day in 1964 when my American family had tried to enter Canada.

The letter told me that because my sister had Down's Syndrome I was not admissible to Canada.

Everyone in the family got a similar letter, including my then five-year-old sister, whose letter told her that because she had Down's Syndrome she was not admissible to Canada.

We went back to Vermont to stay with my grandparents, and the church in Nova Scotia that had hired my father as its new pastor petitioned the government on our behalf. There was a law that stipulated that a foreigner could only be hired to fill a position if no qualified Canadians were available. As the denomination's seminary was located in Boston there were at the time no Canadians with the desired training. We were finally allowed to enter, on the condition that we never become Canadian citizens.

My mother says that in the years before we received permanent resident status every day had been lived in fear of (what was then called) Canada Customs agents coming to the door to deport us again. They'd certainly been given the discretion to do so.

Borders have remained strange and frightening places for me, Canada's no less because of the sometimes stark contrast between border guard comportment and Canadian values. I revisited the trauma of border tyranny when my brother tried to bring his American wife back home, and again years later when I chose to marry a foreigner.

The emotional effect of such experiences is an unstable sense of belonging coupled with a stubborn pride. Exiles have my sympathy. Once excluded from a society one responds to demands for obedience and conformity with a disgruntled, "You shut me out, and so I owe no allegiance to your elitist system, your backward values, your bland tastes, your stifling prudery, or your bizarre class system. Bugger off. I owe you nothing."

This, I've learned, is a good place to be. It means living authentically with who you are as a person. How sweet the realization that music itself knows no borders and that each one of us is welcome to the whole world's smorgasbord of sounds.

And what do we exiles say to those who question our freedom to make the music we want to make?

"Bugger off. I owe you nothing."

Survivor

If some one loves a flower, of which just one single blossom grows, in all the millions and millions of stars, it is enough to make him happy just to look at the stars. He can say to himself, 'Somewhere my flower is there ...'
— Antoine de Sainte-Exupéry

On Christmas Eve, 1998, my husband, my son, and I had attended the evening service. This has always been a precious part of my Christmas, that winter evening ritual with its candles and carols, surrounded by people who'd loved and cared for me since my infancy, whose children and grandchildren I now loved and cared for. My husband had always resented going to church, and I'd encouraged him to stay home this time, but he'd insisted.

Only 20 minutes into the service he began hissing in my ear, "When's this fuckin' gonna be over?" *Calm, calm, it will end soon.* By the end of the service he'd worked himself into such a pique that when I paused to talk to someone on the way out he gave me a hard shove from behind.

When we returned home he went downstairs to his workshop, my son went to his room, and I sat in the living room, looking at the Christmas tree and trying to feel happy. I heard a shriek from downstairs and assumed that my husband had kicked my little dog Spam, as was his wont. I sat there, numb and aching. *Calm, calm, it will end soon.*

He came back upstairs and stood in the doorway, smirking with pride.

"That little bastard won't be getting into *my* cookies again." Yes, he'd kicked Spam. *Calm, calm, it will end soon.*

But the next morning I answered a scratch at the door to find Spam, his neck swollen beyond recognition, still standing but unable to raise his head. I picked him up and carried him downstairs to hold him on my lap in front of the fire, to cry over him and whisper, "I'm so sorry, Spam. This should never have happened to you."

When my husband came downstairs I begged him to take Spam to the vet. He pulled the dog from my arms, took him outside, and shot him, leaving his body on the open ground where I could see it every time I washed dishes.

My baby was due in in a month and a half.

On February 12 my man told me to get out. *Calm, calm, it will end soon.* We lived close to a beautiful woodland path where I would walk each day. It was a phenomenally warm winter, and instead of heaps of snow we had bare ground and a drizzling rain. I walked with our other dog, Christian, until I was exhausted, then returned home, hoping the anger was spent.

He came out to greet me, shouting, "And take your son with you!" before heading back down to the basement. *Calm, calm, it will end soon.*

I was chilled and running a fever. He'd insisted on keeping the heat off upstairs, where I was, while he remained downstairs in his workshop with a stoked wood stove. I was washing dishes when a steady pain entered my abdomen. I called the Digby hospital and they told me to come in. My husband drove me. After examining me my doctor told me everything was fine but that a caesarian might be needed, and there were no surgeons there that night. He ordered an ambulance and had me sent to Yarmouth.

That night I have birth to a beautiful, perfect, eight-and-a-half-pound baby girl whose heartbeat had stopped while she was entering the world.

I knew then that the coming years would be lived in the shadow of what should have been.

We'd already named her La'sel, a Mi'kmaq version of Rachel, which in Hebrew means female lamb. The significance of this name grew as I wrestled with the pain her absence.

A month later the doctor asked me if I wanted to try having another child. I was surprised by my answer.

"What I want," I said, "is to have her back."

"You can't have her back," he gently replied.

"I know. But that doesn't stop it from being the only thing I want."

As someone who'd always struggled with a sense of being basically unlovable it came as a bright epiphany to me that this child should be so precious that no one could ever replace her.

Love really was that big.

Every morning I would hold my daughter's blanket and listen to "My Funny Valentine" by Sarah Vaughan, bawling my eyes out, my tears a libation to the memory of something I'd lost forever but would never stop loving.

Don't change a hair for me,
Not if you care for me.
Stay, little valentine, stay –
Each day is Valentine's Day.
    —*from "My Funny Valentine"*
        by Richard Rodgers and Lorenz Hart, 1937

It was as if a voice from another world was speaking into my life, touching the deepest regions of my emptiness, my hunger for sweetness.

Several months passed before I could begin my day any other way.

If love was big enough for her, it was big enough for me. I would never again need to look to any one person to feel this love. I, too, was unique and irreplaceable. I was loved.

So was everyone.

Mystic

I've heard good arguments refuting the existence of God. I've heard about the "God gene" that predisposes some to believe in a divinity. I've heard profound spiritual experiences explained as psychological phenomena. These arguments all make sense to me. But nothing adequately explains that pesky haunted feeling, that sense of oceanic majesty and oneness with eternity, those experiences of seeing objects in their ideal forms, those life-changing dreams. I can't find anyone offering psychological explanations who's ever claimed to have experienced what I have, and once you've had these kinds of experiences you can't honestly dismiss them as unreal.

I was very religious once, but with time I've come to see prophets and religious institutions as vehicles bringing me to the threshold of the unknowable. Once they'd brought me there it wasn't their business to hang around, and I certainly didn't owe them my devotion.

I'd abandoned devotion to any deity that could be reduced to an archetype, and in the light had come. The light can't be counted, named, or described. Once I knew this I ended up spending far more time in prayer and spiritual study than I had when I'd been "religious."

Music has no place, no form, and no material substance. Music's origins are spiritual, but its manifestation depends, as my flute dream taught me, on three essentials: the human body, earth, and air.

An essential freedom of expression

Marc Vella had pointed to the importance of improvisation as a means of inviting inspiration. Jan Wouter Oostenrijk had told me that notated music was an anomaly and that most cultures play by ear, improvising in such a way that no piece of music can ever really be played the same way twice. Recordings simply froze a particular performance in time, which was a blessing to those of us who couldn't hear the performance in person but in a small way ran counter to an art form which, like the river of Heraclitus, one can never dip one's foot twice in the same place. With recorded music parts of the river may stay the same, but because the listener changes, the experience of listening to a recording changes every time we hear it.

I asked Jason Greenberg, half of the post-rock indie duo In Light Of, for his musical mission statement. He replied, "To try not to control the music stylistically and to do whatever possible to allow it to flow out on its own . . . "

I liked that. Let the music flow. This was not an entirely new idea, but it was one that was getting more attention these days, so it was worth investigating.

Musical effortlessness

The above title must be one of the biggest misnomers in town. Musical effortlessness, at least as explained by the following artists, actually involves far more effort than conventional music practice. But the concept calls for the abolishing of strain, competitiveness, rote memorization, and musical discipline as a military exercise. Musical effortlessness is about none of that; musical effortlessness is *cool*.

There is so much you can learn as a kid, and then when you actually hear someone do what you are learning something clicks, and you think, Oh, it's that easy, or, it's more conceptual than technical. I had a great conducting teacher in school say that it's all concept. He said that you can have all the technique you want, but without concept, you're screwed.

A big influence to me was Kenny Werner. I've studied with him on and off through the years. He wrote the book Effortless Mastery.

— Marco Benevento

The Kenny Werner book soon arrived, with a CD to help with the prescribed meditations. I shared it with Josh Peck and Jack Malmstrom, my bandmates at the time, both of whom remarked after reading it that it had confirmed their instincts.

In the book Werner tells of how one day, after he'd somehow entered some magical zone of zenlike serenity, he'd played "Autumn Leaves" on the piano. Not just any old version of "Autumn Leaves," but "Autumn Leaves" as had never been played before or since, evoking sighs and compliments from listeners. That event set Werner on a path to discover how to cultivate that mysterious power and release it every time he played.

The ability to produce beautiful music has more to do, according to Werner, with your mental, emotional, and spiritual condition than it does with endless repetitions of scales and exercises, or with developing the skill to play difficult passages quickly and without mistakes. You can use technical skill to make music, as computers seem able to do quite easily, but, as Benevento agrees, when it comes to the *most* beautiful sounds, it's all attitude.

I found the same idea in *The Music Lesson* by Victor L. Wooten, a kind of fanciful journey in which the author is visited by a series of mysterious guides who teach him how to be a better bassist. In order to be a good musician, the protagonist learned, you had to be a good human being and believe in yourself. The lessons had to do with getting your priorities straight, staying focussed, burying yourself in music as opposed to whipping yourself into musical submission on an as-needed basis. Making the best music you're capable of means *relaxing and going with the flow*, disciplining yourself to stay in the moment.

Being cool, that is.

Music as a conduit to other worlds

My one strongest religious belief is that there are higher powers and a god or gods, and there is a universal relationship with them and everybody in this world. There are certain things for all of us that help us connect with them. I use music to recognize that.
— Marco Benevento, interview 2009

I feel like the goal of the artist should be to threaten the establishment and question the status quo, all the while projecting love upon the world. Other times I feel like the goal is to derange one's senses enough to somehow glimpse the unknown, never quite being capable of expressing it, but having seen it to at least be better off.
— Ronley Teper, interview 2017

Late in the summer of 2016 Ahmed and I were strolling past Station Parc in Montreal when we happened on an open-air performance by songstress Kiran Ahluwalia.

Formally trained in the Indian classical tradition, Ahluwalia's voice soared and pulsated with meaning. Her husband, Rez Abbasi, played electric guitar in a style richly influenced by Tuareg music. There was also a brilliant *tabla* player and a thrilling, polyrhythmic accordionist.

Ahluwalia had managed to wed Indian music to North African desert blues. I later found out that she called her music, quite appropriately, "Indo-Saharan." The blend was seamless.

Ahluwalia sang in Urdu, introducing each song with a brief synopsis of its translation. One song, she said, was about that evil inner voice that keeps trying to sabotage your growth, and another was about necessity being the mother of enlightenment. Hearing such cerebral messages delivered in this way in an urban park felt electrifying.

It was clear that this woman had a finely honed spiritual consciousness. When I interviewed her by phone a week later I wasn't surprised to learn she was Sikh.

"I find peace when I go to the Sikh temple," she admitted, but – "I have a love-hate relationship with God, a maybe-you-exist, maybe-you-don't kind of a relationship. I believe that we're connected. We can't ignore something horrible that's happening to a group of people without having it come back to affect us negatively."

A secular holiness

I needn't have been baffled by the contrast between the intense spirituality of her music and her pseudo-agnosticism. My own on-again, off-again religious life, prompted by spiritual epiphanies and inevitably doused by encounters with institutionalized religion, had lead me to pursue something I called "secular holiness," that is, a life infused with spiritual meaning, perhaps even full of religious ritual, yet whose allegiance extended beyond religion, surrendering itself to the source of all life and love.

In this context musical expression makes perfect sense; although it can be done explicitly in the name of a religion or ideology, the music's intention and message is above all that. Even music created to promote a particular sacred path or set of ideas can appeal to those who don't share those beliefs. I was raised a Protestant but I'm deeply moved by hymns to Mary, finding meanings perhaps unintended by the authors and singers. One doesn't have to be Muslim to stirred by Sufi music. And the beauty of negro spirituals doesn't lose intensity when it falls on a nonchristian ear.

Sax player Nat Birchall expanded on this idea:

> My belief really is that the music exists independently of our involvement. We are really the conduits for it to reach people. When we play at our best we really play beyond ourselves, and the music happens by itself.
>
> The message or meaning can be felt by the listener but can be interpreted in different ways. It's really a transfer of energies or emotion that happens. It probably goes beyond literal meaning and into empathy or beyond even that sometimes.
>
> The strangest things that have happened have been when the music becomes so profound that it suddenly feels as though you are

listening to someone else playing. You feel unconnected to what's happening and almost as if you are having an out-of-body experience. It's quite rare and doesn't last for very long but is always a very profound moment.

— Nat Birchall, interview 2016

The gospels tell the story of a woman of ill repute, known traditionally as "the magdalen," who entered a home where Jesus was dining. She'd brought with her a jar of spikenard, which was an incredibly expensive perfume. Much to the annoyance of the disciples, who insisted the perfume could have been sold and the money given to the poor, the woman emptied the bottle onto Jesus' feet, washing them with her hair and weeping. Jesus defended her act by saying that we will always have the poor with us, and that she was preparing his body for burial.

This story is a striking reminder of the value of art within spirituality. Art doesn't normally feed the poor, enrich the church's coffers, teach Sunday School, or organize ecumenical conferences, but when it's authentic, art speaks of a love of which most of the world's religious can only dream. Art is the fallen woman, the slave, the exile, the abuse survivor, the mystic, the oppressed, the marginalized, all rising up in an affirmation of love.

Music is thus not just an idle pastime, but a sacrifice of beauty in honour of Love itself.

Mallabozan claimed that music was evidence of the profundity of the human soul: "Music is just translating the soul's feeling to notes," he said, "So I ask myself, 'How great is this soul to have such beauty?'"

The same sentiment was echoed by guitarist Michael Gauthier, who pointed out that animals don't experience sounds the way we do. They'll respond to music but only if trained and don't experience music as distinct from other sounds.

Music lends itself to sacred practice without necessarily being religious, so for spiritual beings who don't follow a religion, music can be the perfect means of expressing the sacredness they feel.

I can be brought to tears when listening to a gospel choir! It's the sheer level of love and belief in our connection through music to the divine, whatever that may mean to the individual, that is so tangible in gospel. Not only gospel of course but so many genres embody a connection to something greater than just the music itself. I believe that this connection, the emotional relationship that we feel, the 'spirituality' that we relate to, is the backbone of our enjoyment of music.
— Graham George, British guitarist, 2018

Translating the soul

In 2016 Christina Enigma of KyAzMa weighed in on the otherworldliness of music:

> The most blown away that I can be is either alone in the living room with my piano, or with Will, deep in a jam. It gets so profound that I've literally broken down in tears with it.
>
> 'Where is it coming from?' I wonder. It's like that openness and allowance of channelling resources, I suppose. This is what I personally strive to bring to others. It may not be as universally opening for everybody as it is for me, but for a lot of people, I think that it has the ability to do that.

In 2017 Mallabozan elaborated:

> Imagine if we could feel each other and discover each other's souls' beauty directly; in that case we wouldn't need a translator between us. We would understand the soul language. Music is just the nearest sound of the soul; we're using music as a vehicle, but if there were even one person who could understand our soul language, we wouldn't need music.

That dark man at the crossroads

Now I know some people, who sold their souls to the devil
And they don't sound nothing, like Robert Johnson!
—Gurf Morlix, from the song "Crossroads"

The ancient Greeks said that when you make a man a slave you take away half his soul.

The dark man at the crossroads only approaches these half-snatched souls . . .

. . . like the slave, the exile, the poor wayfaring stranger, the lonesome cowpoke.

The dark man isn't the devil's henchman.

It's an angel sent to fill the broken soul with the beauty of a magical, primal sound.

Right now my most oft-visited crossroads is the Montreal metro. I've found many musicians there offering up their sacrifices of beauty, and I sometimes video them as I'm walking by. The great stone archways of the underground provide a resonant, ringing sound to even the gentlest troubadour, and artists range from solitary off-key voices singing in distant tongues to brilliant one-person bands playing four instruments at once.

In order to get home on the Montreal metro I generally have to get off the orange line at Jean Talon to get onto to blue line, which takes me to Fabre. When I leave the orange line it feels like I'm descending into the bowels of the earth, deeper, deeper, to find the landing for the blue line to St. Michel. The music and the depth make this particular crossroads especially evocative.

One day I'd made it down to the blue line and was waiting quietly. I was deeply depressed, having acquired the conviction that I was lost finally and would never find my way "back home." I soon noticed that nearby a middle-aged man with a backpack was singing, in the most incredibly beautiful, lyrical voice. I believe he was singing in Spanish, and although I don't know Spanish I was pretty sure it was a love song. I looked into his eyes to find him looking into mine with an innocent tenderness beyond imagining. His eyes carried a message: *Yes, love really is that big.*

My depair melted away like cotton candy in a rainstorm. It occurred to me that this man might be an angel. I looked around to see if anyone else had noticed him. No one seemed aware of his presence despite the continual singing, but they might just have been acting with typical urban coldness to this unusual phenomenon. I considered asking the young man near me if he could see the singing man, but thought better of it. I would cherish the memory of this man as an angel whether he was or not, because that's what he'd been for me. He hadn't asked for my soul; he'd given me a song to fill the emptiness of my own.

My underground crossroads experience gave me cause to reflect: What happens once the archetypal artist approaches the archetypal crossroads in search of her stolen soul and has it then returned to her stronger, lovelier, and more divine?

I imagine she becomes a dervish. The crossroads being such a potent symbol of the intersection of the sacred with the profane, the soul standing at that intersection now complete can enter a state of mystical turning that, incorporating all, transcends all. The soul's whirling is a perpetual state of worship and gratitude, a trance state that enters the mundane and fills it with a holy fragrance: the assurance of an essential freedom.

But an essential compenet is being ignored here: The sky. The sky with lights and waters overspilling, the sky to which the whirling dervish, drunk on love, ascends, the sky from which the lovely dark angel comes and to which it will soon return, the sky which is the great zero, the encompassing symbol of the spirit world that birthed us and that will one day welcome us home, the sky whose image of a round horizon sits atop the Tuareg cross, a sign of who we are and of the divine power granted us and required of us.

Echoes of earth's heart

Bear River Band Hall, late winter, 2000: The drummers are singing "The Grandmother Song," a traditional Mi'kmaq summons to the ancestors of everyone in the room. Looking around at the assortment of ethnic groups represented here, I imagine our ancestors all showing up at once. I worry about how they'll all get along.

We're seated on low stools around the drum – a massive hollowed oak tree trunk with a moose hide stretched across its surface. We continue pounding until 11:30 pm, when Dusty tells us that if we continue to drum past midnight we'll be obliged to drum all night long.

As rife with taboos as drumming appears to be, the admonition sounds suspiciously convenient for a father of four who needs his rest. No one could fault him: Dusty has given up his few leisure hours to explain traditional drumming to a few friends, using these drumming sessions as introductions to Mi'kmaq spirituality.

One of the first things we learn is that the drumbeat echoes the heartbeat of Mother Earth. Recreating her heartbeat is a sacred ritual, an act that sets us within nature and outside it at the same time. The drum isn't an idol to be worshipped but rather a vehicle of spiritual experience, and followers of diverse religions are free to use it.

There's a significant – and measurable – value in such rituals. In 1994 an interesting study[17] conducted in British Columbia showed that although First Nations communities in that province had a higher than average adolescent suicide rate, the communities that promoted their traditional cultures and participated in traditional practices like drumming actually had a lower rate of teen suicide than in the population at large.

It would seem, at least according to this study, that traditional cultural practices may be effective antidotes to the harmful aftereffects of colonial oppression. But why? A prevailing theory holds that our mental health requires a solid sense of self and that in order to develop one we need to see ourselves as part of a continuity, ideally a part of something that's been around for a long time and will probably be around for a long time to come.

If similar studies could be conducted in non-aboriginal communities I'm sure we'd see that participation in traditional musical practices correlates with good mental health. The current popularity of drum circles in diverse ethnic groups, drawing forth testimonies of enlightenment, balance, and enhanced energy, is one indication of the continuing importance of this ancient musical practice.

I've already talked about the magical serendipity of making music communally, but when the music we're making is as primal as drumming we've entered an alternate reality, summoning the dreamworld to help us on our way.

Making music, in particular carrying on the music of one's ancestors, has a mysterious balancing and grounding power that can help get us through addiction, depression, suicidal ideation, and other psychosocial dilemmas. It can lead us to the kind of wholeness Abraham Maslow talks about in his "hierarchy of needs." Music is spiritual in origin and tends to steer us toward its spiritual sources.

Surely in this vortical journey primal music carries a message from the past forward to the living.

---

17   https://journals.sagepub.com/doi/abs/10.1177/136346159803500202

A relentless demand for reconciliation

Justin Trudeau's 24th of November (2016) apology on behalf of Canada to survivors of residential schools in Labrador and Newfoundland raised public consciousness regarding the relentless nature of the First Nations' demand for reconciliation. Reparations weren't enough; there had to be an expression of regret and an observable effort to keep it from happening again.

If you've ever felt compelled to ask someone for an apology you'll know it doesn't often go well. Their refusal to express remorse will pretty much spell the end of the relationship. After all, if they're not sorry now, nothing's to stop them doing it again. Why would you keep putting your heart out there to get stomped on? Whatever love you may have held for that person, the sensible solution is to start moving that love in another direction, at last for now.

But a few First Nations people of Newfoundland and Labrador didn't give up, and eventually the apology came. Their perseverance carried an implicit but stirring gist: *We value this relationship enough to do what it takes to make it work, even if that means compelling you to do something you don't like.*

Those few exceptional human beings were surely drumming while they waited for that apology. The political urge toward reconciliation was an echo of the drum's call to peace, of the Grandmother Song calling all of us to reach down into our roots for the strength to make things right in the world of the living.

Coming to the fore

Music filled my sense of emptiness as it has for millennia filled the emptiness of the slave, the poor, the refugee, the prisoner, the exile. A presence was singing me through it all. It was this presence that dictated that for the next 20 years my life would in one way or another revolve around music.

Composer-producer Lex Norwood was in New York to witness an explosion of musical talent being ignored in favour of mindless commercial drivel. When he spoke of this period in his life the discouragement was still palpable in his voice. But when asked what music meant to him, he had this to say:

> Music is something personal that God gave to us as human beings to comfort us in troubled times. When we're frustrated there are a couple of things we can go to: vices or music. To be honest you can still go to music tanked up on something, but we turn on some music anyway. For me I think He gave me the gift to cope with life.
> — Lex Norwood, interview 2019

This sentiment — that the music business falls short but music remains precious — is as real for nonbelievers as it is for believers, albiet couched in a different lingo. Greek opera singer Christos Stassinoploulos, an avowed agnostic, puts it this way:

> I've never had the chance to experience any ideal conditions, so I can't say for sure what ideal conditions for creativity would be. The only certain thing I can say is that music has always been my small window to light even during the darkest moments of my life.
> — Christos Stassinopoulos, interview 2010

I'm deeply grateful for the privilege of living through this era and for the words of so many wise music makers. And knowing that all of music can be present to me at every moment makes me feel like a host of caroling angels is carrying me o'er the tumult. (At the moment the soundtrack is Norwood's "God's Speed," an instrumental throbbing with the assurance of the smile behind the world's pain.)

I love what Mallabozan says:

> I remember in 2007 I deeply believed that if the whole people on the earth will make a protest against God and will ask him to speak to us and let us hear his voice, I was so sure his voice would be melodies, and the sounds will be exactly the Oud sound.

Swiss composer-producer Blaise Caillet expressed our essential safeness when describing his album's cover image – a snail on a razor's edge:

> We're all snails coming up to a razor edge. But do you know what happens to a snail on a razor edge? Nothing! His body and skin type allow him to rest on a razor's edge, or on anything sharp or prickly, without getting hurt!
> —Blaise Caillet of SKNAIL, interview 2016

The same idea is expressed in Horatio Spafford's 1876 hymn "It is Well With My Soul:"

> When peace like a river attended my way,
> When sorrows like sea billows roll,
> Whatever my lot
> Thou hast taught me to say,
> 'It is well, it is well with my soul.'

In some mysterious way we're all safe, and remembering this empowers us to find meaning in this vale of tears. Music is our reminder.

My soundquest isn't over. Soon some exquisite sound will thrill me and off I'll go in search of its essence. The last 20 years have lead me to the decision to spend more time making music and composing, wherever that might lead. I know that the same spectre will greet me in the end: a dervish at the crossroads wailing his pain to heaven and, like the psalmist, finishing his plaint with a universal hymn of praise that sends him swirling skyward:

How blessed is this broken world, how blessed!

References and inspiration

Arendt, Hannah. *The Life of the Mind: The Groundbreaking Investigation on How We Think*. Open Road Integrated Media, 1981. Scribd. Web. July 2018.

Byrne, David. *How Music Works,* Recorded Books Audio. 2012. Scribd. Web. March 2018.

Doggett, Peter. *There's a Riot Going On: Revolutionaries, Rock Stars, and the Rise and Fall of the '60s*. Canongate Books, 2007. Print.

Herstand, Ari. *How To Make It in the New Music Business: Practical Tips on Building a Loyal Following and Making a Living as a Musician*. High-Bridge Audio, November 2016. Scribd. Web. October 2018.

Johnson , Ian. *A Mosque in Munich: Nazis, the CIA, and the Rise of the Muslim Brotherhood in the West*. Mariner Books, May 2010. Scribd. Web. 2014.

Jung, Carl, *Memories, Dreams, and Reflections,* New York: Vintage, 1965. Print.

Levitin, Daniel J. *Your Brain on Music: The Science of a Human Obsession*. Penguin Random House Audio, 2007. Scribd. Web. November 2017.

Maritain, Jacques, *Art and Scholasticism, and the Frontiers of Poetry,* Scribner 1962. Print.

Nietzsche, Friedrich. *The Birth of Tragedy*. AB Publishing Audio, 2016. Scribd. Web. February 2019.

Schneider, Jason. *Whispering Pines: The Northern Roots of American Music ... From Hank Snow to The Band*. ECW Press, July 2009. Scribd. Web. October 2018.

Werner, Kenny. *Effortless Mastery: Liberating the Master Musician Within*. New Albany, IN: Jamey Abersold Jazz, Inc., 1996. Print.

Witt, Stephen. *How Music Got Free: The End of an Industry, the Turn of the Century, and the Patient Zero of Piracy,* Penguin Random House Audio, 2015. Scribd. Web. January 2018.

Wooten, Victor L. *The Music Lesson: A Spiritual Search for Growth Through Music*. Tantor Audio, 2010. Scribd. Web. February 2018.

Yarshater, Ehsan, ed., *Mystical Poems of Rumi*. Chicago: The University of Chicago Press, 1979. Print.

About the author

WANDA WATERMAN'S poetry has been published in *Descant, Pottersfield Portfolio, Tigertail,* and *Our Times,* and her articles in *The New Internationalist* and *This Magazine.* She's worked as an independent music journalist since 2005. After having grown up in Nova Scotia and living in New Hampshire and Tunisia she's now settled in Montreal, where she writes and makes music with people from all over the world. *Dervish at the Crossroads* is her first published book.